ONE NATION UNDER GOD

Biblical Backing for Christian Voters

DAVID BOUDREAUX

PROISLE PUBLISHING

© Copyright 2024 by David Boudreaux

ISBN: 978-1-963735-45-1

All rights reserved. No part of this book may be reproduced or transmitted in any form or by any means, electronic or mechanical, including photocopying, recording, or by any information storage and retrieval system, without permission in writing from the copyright owner.

The views expressed in this work are solely those of the author and do not necessarily reflect the views of the publisher, and the publisher disclaims any responsibility for them.

To order additional copies of this book, contact:

Proisle Publishing Services LLC
39-67 58th Street, 1st floor
Woodside, NY 11377, USA
Phone: (+1 646-480-0129)
info@proislepublishing.com

I feel like King Solomon when he became King over Israel and God told Solomon to ask Him for whatever he wanted. King Solomon only asked God for wisdom II Chronicles 1:10. May God be our guide as we ponder the decision that will lead America into the future.

THE PLEDGE OF ALLEGIANCE

I pledge allegiance to the flag of the United States of America, and to the Republic for which it stands ***one Nation under God***, indivisible, with liberty and justice for all.

Table of Contents

CHAPTER 1 — The Current State of America ---------- 1

CHAPTER 2 — Religious Freedom Under Attack ------- 7

CHAPTER 3 — A How-To-Win Strategy --------------- 13

CHAPTER 4 — Christian Perspective ------------------- 21

CHAPTER 5 — Democratic Socialism ------------------ 34

CHAPTER 6 — Same Sex Marriage --------------------- 38

CHAPTER 7 — Terrorism ------------------------------ 46

CHAPTER 8 — Supporting The Military --------------- 53

CHAPTER 9 — Illegal Immigration -------------------- 58

CHAPTER 10 – The National Debt -------------------- 66

CHAPTER 11 – Stop Lawlessness --------------------- 70

CHAPTER 12 – The Right To Bear Arms -------------- 75

CHAPTER 13 – The Drug Crisis ----------------------- 81

CHAPTER 14 – The Solution To The Drug Crisis ----- 90

CHAPTER 15 – Student Debt Forgiveness ----------- 106

CHAPTER 16 – Climate Change --------------------- 111

CHAPTER 17 – The Economy ------------------------ 120

CHAPTER 18 – Summary And Conclusion ----------- 128

CHAPTER ONE
THE CURRENT STATE OF AMERICA

THE LEGISLATION OF IMMORALITY

For those of us who profess to be Christians, religion and politics are intertwined with each other and therefore inseparable. I am not willing to admit that America is no longer a Christian nation as President Obama once proclaimed, but if we want America to remain a Christian nation that is blessed by God, then all Christians must become more politically active. It amazes me that so many of today's generation are so uneducated concerning the political realm that they have neither the knowledge, nor the desire, to cast an informed vote. Polls have shown that approximately only 26% of Christians, or evangelicals as we are often referred to, voted in 2008 and 2012, while 78% voted in 2004. Many say that they are not going to vote because the election process is corrupt and their vote will not count anyhow. All I can say to that is no system is perfect, but one thing is certain, what we have been doing, (not voting) is definitely not working. For the first time in the history of America, beginning during the Obama administration, Christians are being prosecuted and sent to jail for practicing their scriptural beliefs and the Supreme Court is now legislating immorality in the name of civil rights. I want to share with you an article that I authored and posted online a couple of years ago which illustrates the severity of the political issues at hand. This article should assist you in determining whether you want to read this book or not because it illustrates how I believe a Christian should base his or her life on the Word Of God, and if that is not the kind of Christian that you are, then this book is not going to be for you.

AM I STILL IN AMERICA

"I never thought I would see what I am seeing take place in America. When Obama lit up the white house with rainbow colors I felt like it was a sign that America had taken a significant turn toward the dark side and I began to wonder how long it would take for God to turn His back on us. I often hear that the Word of God is somewhat vague in numerous areas concerning morality issues, but one thing is sure. God is not vague at all concerning homosexuality. I suppose it was only a matter of time until human rights would over-ride morality, but still I never thought I would see it get to this point. The first thing you hear from politicians is that you can't legislate morality, but I can't believe that now we are legislating immorality. Christians are not passing judgement on people as they are often accused, however they are commissioned by God to pass judgement on what is right and wrong concerning moral issues. They feel as though they have a moral responsibility to share with the world what they have learned from the Word of God concerning what is right and wrong and what the consequences are of disobeying God. Christians don't claim to be free from sin and yet if they try to warn someone about what God says out of love they are immediately condemned and discredited by having their past sins exposed to the world. Two wrongs don't make a right. No Christian is trying to proclaim that they are without sin; they are simply trying to warn the rest of humanity not to make the same mistakes that they have. Whether we believe it or not there are consequences for immorality whether these offenses are committed as an individual are as a nation. Christians are not saying they are any better than anyone else, they are admitting that all people are sinners and fall short of the glory of God. The only difference between Christians and non-Christians is the fact that Christians (through the shed blood of Jesus Christ) have had their sins forgiven in the sight of God and non-Christians have not. When the Christians ask God to forgive them of their sins they are forgiven for past, present and future sins because they are not asking for forgiveness of a particular sin, but rather they are asking to be forgiven for being a sinner. So therefore to assume that Christians are claiming to be sinless is wrong. They are admitting that they are sinners just like everyone else. Am I still in America is the question I am asking because I never thought we would send someone to jail in America for being moral. Does anyone still believe in following God's Word in this Country? As a Christian, I do not desire to push my views on someone else. When I tell someone that God says what they are doing is immoral I am doing it out of love not hate. If I saw someone about to drive over a bridge that I knew was unsafe to drive on and I didn't try to warn them of the danger should I feel partially responsible for what happens to them? This is how a Christian feels when he sees someone headed down an immoral path of destruction.

They say that you can't mix religion and politics; does that only apply when religion is trying to prevent immorality, or is it also applicable when politics tries to silence religion? The fact is you can not separate religion and law. Anyone ever notice the similarities between the Laws that God laid down in His Word and the laws that we follow in America? Duh! We do legislate morality in this country because that is where the majority of our laws originated. So now we are prosecuting Christians for following the blueprint that our laws came from. It is one thing for the Supreme Court to pass laws that are contrary to God's laws (that is bad enough) but now we are sending Christians to jail for being moral. I am not trying to discriminate against anyone; I am simply telling it the same way the Word of God does. If someone is offended then I feel they should not be taking it personally because God said what they are doing is wrong long before they started doing it. Christians are not judging the person committing the act, that is between the person doing it and God. What they are doing is reminding the world that God told us a long time ago that this is an immoral act. Don't get mad at the Christians for trying to warn you. If you want to get mad at someone get mad at God because He is the one that said it was an immoral act, not the Christian. Was Obama right when he said that America is no longer a Christian nation? I hope he wasn't because I fear the consequences if this is true. It is time for American Christians to take a stand and proclaim enough is enough. By the way, it really doesn't matter if you believe the Word of God or not, the consequences for immorality remain the same.

God has been very good to this nation and I for one, believe it is because we have been a moral nation. Now that we have started prosecuting morality instead of immorality how do you think God is looking at us?"

A GODLESS NATION

So you see, Christians must get educated and get involved in politics and vote because when a nation is run by Godless politicians, it becomes a Godless nation. If the Christians in this country want to reverse this Godless path that we are headed down, then we must be able to choose a presidential candidate that will represent Christianity. This is a candidate that will support laws that are based on Scripture and not laws that ignore Scripture in the name of human rights. Are the laws of the created (mankind) more relevant than the Laws of the Creator (God)? You can be sure that many of the topics that we will cover in this political discussion have been and will continue to be controversial. Edmund Burk's statement "All that is necessary for the triumph of evil is for good men to do nothing" has never been more applicable. The reason our country is in the position that it is in is because good men have done nothing to stop it. In my opinion, the Obama administration and current administration are good examples of wolves in sheep's clothing. They have consistently enforced laws, passed executive orders, ignored existing laws and made judgement calls that are contrary to the Word of God. They have done this under the guise of human rights and civil rights, but their agenda is perfectly clear. The reason they are doing this is because this is how they will win votes and maintain power. A democratic society must be run by enforcing moral laws not by popularity among the people. The reason that immorality is considered to be more popular is because the moral people that built this country have remained voiceless. The fact is that all judicial laws are designed for the purpose of protecting people from harming themselves or others. People who live by God's laws do not need man's laws to prevent them from harming anyone. In fact, those who have the love of God inside them don't even need God's laws to do the right thing. Look at the following verses:

> Knowing this, that the law is not made for a righteous man, but for the lawless and disobedient, for the ungodly and for sinners, for unholy and profane, for murderers of fathers and murderers of mothers, for manslayers, For whoremongers, for them that defile themselves with mankind, for menstealers, for liars, for perjured persons, and if there be any other thing that is contrary to sound doctrine; According to the glorious gospel of the blessed God, which was committed to my trust. (I Tim 1:9-11)

Chapter Two
Religious Freedom under Attack

Christians Have Rights Too

It has been suggested by the liberal media that it is discriminatory for a business owner to refuse to accommodate certain individuals request even if it is against their religious beliefs to do so. If Christians are not allowed to conduct themselves in a manner that is considered acceptable to their faith, then what is the meaning of religious freedom? If that is true, then is it discriminatory to prosecute a thief for stealing? That sounds like a ridiculous argument, but I have known some people in my lifetime that were professional thieves and they did not feel like there was anything wrong with stealing. What happens if the majority of the people in this country start to feel that way? Will we make it legal to be a thief because that is what the majority of the people want? Laws cannot be based on what certain groups consider to be acceptable. To prove that this idea is not all that far out there, we still have laws on the books that say sex outside of marriage is illegal, but today it is considered acceptable in most circles and therefore the laws are considered a joke and are routinely ignored. It hasn't been that long ago when everyone thought it was wrong and was something to be ashamed of. With this in mind, when will being a professional thief be considered acceptable behavior just because everyone is doing it? I was watching a movie just yesterday that actually suggested this very thing. They proclaimed that stealing is considered normal behavior in today's society and is to be expected. What about drugs? Not too long ago drugs were considered a crime by everyone, but because of their popularity now they are legal in many states. These things were wrong in God's Word in the beginning and they still are.

INCOME EQUALITY

A prime example of this is the fact that there are more people in this country on welfare, unemployment and food stamps than ever before. This seems, on the surface, to be a good thing, our government is more willing than ever to help those in need, but the problem is too many of these beneficiaries are taking advantage of the system. Our nearly 33 trillion dollar deficit should be proof enough that this type of redistribution of wealth is not sustainable. This deficit has grown substantially in just the last few years and was only 19 trillion in 2015. Income equality is the term that is misused to justify this non-sense. In America, we already have income equality for the most part. Every person is free to educate and prepare themselves for the ability to earn as much income as they are personally capable of, if they are willing to work for it. Income equality should not mean if you are not willing to work for it, then the government is going to take it from someone who did work for it and give it to you. This is socialism and if you think our current monetary system of distribution is unfair, then wait until it is up to the government to determine how much of the money you earned you are allowed to keep and how much you are required to give to those who refuse to work. Socialism under any other name (Democratic Socialism) is still socialism. When a person is perfectly capable of working, but simply refuses to do so because the Government is offering to pay them more to stay home than they can make working, then the system is run amuck. What does God say?

> If a man will not work then neither should he eat. (II Thes 3:10)

SOCIALISM IS NOT SUSTAINABLE

This may sound harsh on the surface, but no nation can sustain a society of people who will not work. America is a great nation because our laws have been based on morals. That is the way our founders envisioned it and the way those generations before us have preserved it. America is great because we are a capitalistic society that encourages people to work and to be proud. In today's society, the only time we can feel proud to be an American is when we see a small military victory against our enemies, (which is increasingly rare) or when we watch an NRA (National Rifleman's Association) commercial on TV. I am not even sure at this point, that the current administration still knows who our enemies are and who our allies are. When we have made a deal with Iran, who is a sworn enemy of America and one of our greatest allies Israel, it makes one wonder. America cannot survive another four years of politics as usual regardless of who our next president is. The majority of the American politicians today no longer represents the desires of the people, but rather base their positions on partisan politics, the demands of their special interest groups or the request of lobbyist. Our governmentally enforced policies are formed around buying votes, political advancement or financial greed.

BUYING VOTES

The refusal of this administration to enforce immigration laws is not based on American traditional generosity, as certain public officials would have you believe, it is simply a policy devised to please a large number of people whom have broken the law in an effort to convince them to vote a certain way. I know you will say that illegal immigrants cannot vote. My reply to that would be Legally first and Not yet secondly. This fact became evident with the push from the left to give illegal immigrants driver's licenses and to fight the efforts to require a picture ID in order to vote. They claimed that this effort to require an ID would be discriminatory causing a hardship for the poor. That argument doesn't hold water since the ID is free. Then they said that issuing a license to illegal immigrants would keep the roads safe. Personally, I don't believe they are concerned about how safe the roads are. Keeping illegal immigrants out of the country would do the same thing. The truth is if they don't have to prove that they are legal citizens to vote, then they are free to vote in favor of the party that promotes illegal immigration. The plan is if they have a valid driver's license, then they meet the ID requirement and can still vote. Politics is all about money and power. I am sure that all Americans want our nation to be generous and to be great again, but this will not be accomplished by rewarding lawlessness.

IMPORTING VOTES

If a political party can't win the elections by receiving enough votes from legal citizens, then they will import votes through illegal immigration. Let me be perfectly clear here, I do not fault the immigrants for this fiasco. If I were in their position I would do the same thing they are doing, but as an American citizen, I want our laws and policies to be based on what the American people want, not the opinion of non-citizens. I must emphasize that I do not have a problem with legal immigration what so ever. I believe every person should have the same rights that American born citizens have, but the fact is that even America cannot afford to accommodate what should be the rights of every person born on the earth. In order to afford those rights to our own citizens, both those born here, and those who have migrated legally, there must remain certain restrictions to the immigration process. Open boarders are not an option if we as a nation intend to continue to offer those rights to our own. America, after all, does have the most lenient and most generous immigration policies of any country in the world already. I am aware that taking a stand on these issues will automatically open me to personal attacks since that is how those with an opposing opinion will try to invalidate these conservative views. I don't care about that because I have already admitted to being far from perfect. I have committed many sins against the Word of God in my lifetime, but that doesn't change the fact that the things that are sins for me are still sins for everyone else as well. By definition, a sin is voluntarily committing those acts that are contrary to the teachings of God and we have all done that and continue to do that every day. My life is literally an open book. I wrote an entire book about the wrong things that I have done so go ahead and feel free to attack. I have never made a claim to be a perfect person and neither are you. "Let he who is without sin cast the first stone" (Jn 8:7)

Chapter Three
A How-to-Win Strategy

Electability

One of the things that must be considered when choosing a presidential candidate is electability. By that I mean even if we as evangelicals have chosen a person whom meets all of our criteria for the perfect person to steer us back on the right course, what are the chances that during a general election that person can actually win a majority of the vote in the country? We have to admit that in our society today there are a large number of people who are not informed well enough in the political realm to make the wisest choices concerning the right leader. There are many in our society who do not care about the direction that the country is going morally and only care about their personal agendas. There are those who will only vote for the party that has traditionally supported unions, or gay rights, or abortion rights, or civil rights even though that may no longer be true. Then there are those who have been raised in what has been termed as "A yellow dog Democrat" family. That simply means that their family has always voted straight Democrat regardless of who is on the ticket. In their minds they have fulfilled their duty as an American citizen by casting their vote, but they really have no idea about the agendas of the people they have voted for. To quote a popular song, "The only thing that stays the same is everything changes". Today's Democratic Party is no-where near what it used to be. The

Democratic Party of the yester-years held views that were very similar to what the Republican Party's views are today. Many of today's Democrats have views that are so far left that most people in America can't relate to what they are saying, but it doesn't matter because most Americans don't follow politics and have no idea anyhow.

On the other hand, there are some Republican Party members that are so far to the right that they could be considered extremist. My purpose in this book is to help you, as a conservative Christian voter, decide how you will determine who to vote for, and not to tell you who to vote for. It amazes me that the populous is so uneducated and uninterested in American politics when there are actually few things that matter as much while we are still here on this earth. This is what determines what kind of nation we will have and live in. Many of the college students in America can't even tell you who the Vice President is and have no clue which Party Ronald Reagan or Abraham Lincoln was in. Just for the record, President Lincoln was the first Republican President. So it is a balancing act trying to select someone who will represent the evangelicals adequately and yet can still be elected in a general election. Many people will vote on a candidate based on their like-ability with no regard for their belief system or policy platform. For case-in-point I want to share with you another article that I recently wrote about one of the Republican candidates. This article was published on the internet media LinkedIn back in 2015.

THE REPUBLICAN PARTY HAS BEEN TRUMPED

"Let's face it; Donald Trump has certainly upset the Republican Party with his brash style of politically incorrect speech. Many of us are excited that someone finally has the nerve to publicly state the facts as they really are. It is a fact that China, Mexico and Japan, along with numerous other countries have long taken advantage of America's generous trade policies and we could use someone who truly knows how to negotiate better deals. It is true that many of our policies concerning immigration and anchor babies are antiquated and need to be revised. It is true that Obama care is destroying our health care system and must be dealt with. It is true that Isis is a major problem and if we don't go there and take care of it, it will come to us. It is true that the American economy is in a bad state and all indications are it is not going to get any better anytime soon. It is true that most politicians are already bought and payed for before they ever get into office and therefore they are bound by their agreements with supporters on all major issues and cannot represent the people.

Many have criticized his remarks concerning these issues saying that he is not telling us how he will fix them. The fact is that he is saying more about these issues than any other candidate and many people are listening. The American people want to have a reputation for being generous and kind in the world we live in but we are tired of being walked on. Perhaps at times harsh words are what we need for the world to hear us again. Obama's "leading from behind" policies have left the entire world laughing at us. Our allies don't trust us to follow through with any promise we make, (and they shouldn't). Our enemies no longer put any stock in our threats, (and they shouldn't). Our trade partners believe that we will do anything we have to make a deal and so do our enemies. We have made deals with our enemies that only show the rest of the world that we are more than willing to turn our back on our closest allies to get what we want. Why are we doing this? Is it because we have spent all of our resources giving it to people who either don't care about us at all or we have squandered it on social programs in an effort to buy votes? Everything is about money and power in politics. A large number of the American people are excited that finally there is someone running for President that cannot be bought.

The question is how much of what Mr. Trump says he can do, can really be done. It is a fact that President Obama has set a new standard in acting alone to change existing laws and enact new ones to shove his agenda down our throats, like it or not. He has been challenged in court several times but for the conservatives the court is stacked against us at this time. Is Trump planning to push his agenda in the same way? What is happening in America is lawlessness. It is happening on the streets and in Washington at the highest levels. Can Trump deport 11 million illegal immigrants? Can he fix the broken economy? Can he change the bad trade deals? Can he keep other countries from manipulating the currency? Can he rebuild our weak economy and strengthen our military? Can he make Mexico build a wall? Can he fix a broken IRS that targets certain organizations that lean toward conservatism? Can he make our allies, and even more important our enemies respect us again? Can he fix the problems that have plagued the Veterans Administration for years?

The fact is many of these things cannot be accomplished by the President alone and in many cases he will be fighting extremely liberal democrats (such as the majority on the supreme court) and somewhat moderate conservatives in the congress that have already been bought. Yes, we like what he is saying but can it be done like he claims? Many folks like the fact that he is not a politician, so do I, but just because he knows how to get things done in business doesn't mean he knows how to get things done in politics. I have heard people say "He must know how to do something, he is a billionaire). I must admit that is true but running a company and running a country is not the same thing. The next question, is he presidential in his actions? When he goes online and tweets such things as "I see Megyn is back, I liked the Kelly File much better without her, maybe she should take another unscheduled vacation". Those are not the exact words but essentially it is what he said. I don't care if he likes Megyn Kelly or not. He has made numerous foul comments directed towards her and everyone else that asks difficult questions concerning his controversial position on numerous topics. These are the kinds of defensive statements that are made when someone is backed in a corner by being asked a question that they are not prepared for. Are these types of comments presidential? It is alright when you are just dealing with the press but is this the way we want our president to respond to other world leaders. He says we don't have time to be politically correct. I think political correctness has gotten way out of hand, as do most American citizens, but there is a difference between political correctness and just completely rude and condescending.

I'm not suggesting that anyone should vote for Trump or not, I'm just saying we need to look at everything. In my opinion there are many other viable candidates with great ideas that are not being talked about. Consider Mike Huckabee, perhaps the politician with the most common sense approach to the IRS problem. Consider Fiorina with the best approach to defeat the policies of Hillary or Biden. Consider Ted Cruise with the strongest stand against politics as usual in Washington. Consider Jeb Bush with perhaps the clearest understanding of Planned Parenthood and foreign policy. Consider Ben Carson with the best understanding of our nation's social problems and good ideas concerning rebuilding the military. I know we need a real change in Washington and there are a number of candidates that can make those needed changes. Maybe a non-politician is a good idea and maybe not."

YOU MUST BE PROPERLY INFORMED

This article was written in 2015 and obviously the next election will present new candidates with new ideas, but the principles have not changed. Basically what I am saying is that there are numerous things to consider and I cannot suggest that you vote for a particular candidate. I can only point out the importance of being properly informed and actually going out and making your voice heard through the only avenue made available to us. We must vote to be heard! Just remember it doesn't do any good if we succeed in nominating a perfect leader if he never has the opportunity to lead. I think a candidate's religious affiliation is of considerable significance, but it is most certainly not the only thing that should be weighed in the balance. The reason it is important is because only a Christian will have the same political views and convictions as the conservative Christian. There are obviously many different Christian religions with many different beliefs, but the one thing that ties us all together is accepting Christ as our Lord and Savior which makes us all part of the Body of Christ and a member of the Universal Church of Christ. I think we all need to put aside our petty differences and come together in unity as one large universal Christian voice that cannot be ignored. It will be up to the Christians to save our nation from destruction. If we don't get God back on our side He will allow our enemies to destroy us.

CHAPTER FOUR
CHRISTIAN PERSPECTIVE

BY WHAT AUTHORITY

You may be wondering by now what is it that gives me authority to write such a book as this since I am not a politician. I think the best authority that I have is what I just said, I am not a politician. In America politicians are supposed to represent the people. The Government should be by the people, of the people and for the people. I am not a political scholar. I am just a typical American working class individual. Well, first I am an American citizen that is concerned about the direction our country is headed in. As I am sure you have noticed by now, I am a conservative Christian that believes what the Word of God says and the warnings to individuals and nations of the end results of a nation that turns its back on God. Since the day I became a born again Christian I have followed politics closely paying particular attention to our nation's leadership. It is my opinion that in the last eleven years our country has made a nose dive on numerous fronts toward a path of destruction. President Trump gave some relief on some of those fronts, but he was not able to repair all the damage that the previous administration created. If we stay on this course we will go down in history as a once great nation that was brought down by its refusal to acknowledge God and His Word. I am an ordained minister and I do have a B. A. degree in Pastoral Theology. The one thing that gives me the authority to write this book however, has nothing to with me. The thing that gives me the authority is the same thing that gives all Christians the authority and that is the Word of God.

I believe all of us as Christians have the right and even the responsibility to do all that we can to warn the people in our country about the path that we are headed down as a nation and each of us should use every avenue and every God given ability that we have to get this message out. As I mentioned before, a candidate's religious affiliation is important, but putting religion aside, Christians must make their choices based on which candidate will lead our country down the right path. This path will be determined by his or her beliefs and his or her policies. Not all candidates will have the same religious beliefs that we prefer, some may not even have a religion, but they still may have policies that lead us in the right direction. God says we are to be in this world, but not of this world (John 17:14-15). If you are a dedicated Christian, then you have noticed that the majority of the world does not see things the same way that you do. There are many things that I will do and will not do because I believe God's Word and often times many of my friends just do not understand my thinking. God also says for those to whom much is given, much shall be required (Luke 12:48). God is the one that gave me the ability to publish this warning and therefore I am required to deliver.

WHAT SHOULD OUR VOTES BE BASED ON?

We have to base our votes on policies that lead our country back to God regardless of the religious affiliation of the individual that promotes them. The way we judge these policies is by comparing them with the Word of God. I want to remind the reader of the Scriptural reasons why we believe the way we do concerning such policies. A Christian is someone who is a follower of Christ. This is someone who practices Christianity on a daily basis not just when it is convenient. President Biden was once asked how he could say he was a Christian and still support abortion. I don't recall the exact words, but his reply basically consisted of his proclamation that his religion (Catholicism) taught that abortion was wrong, but he could not allow his religion to interfere with his political policies. This is not the kind of person that represents Christianity in the least. Today, Catholicism is one of the least restrictive religions in the world concerning its convictions and yet they still know that abortion is murder.

PRO-LIFE (ABORTION)

> Before I formed you in the womb I knew you, before you were born I set you apart. (Jer 1:5)
>
> Even before I was Born, God had chosen me to be His. (Gal 1:15)
>
> For You created my inmost being; You knit me together in my mother's womb.... Your eyes saw my unformed body. All the days ordained for me were written in Your

> Book before one of them came to be. (Ps 139:13, 16)
>
> Your hands shaped me and made me… did You not clothe me with skin and flesh and knit me together with bones and sinews? You gave me life. (Job 10:8-12)
>
> This is what the Lord says – He Who made you, Who formed you in the womb. (Is 44:2)
>
> Did not He Who made me in the womb make them? Did not the same One form us both within our mothers? (Job 31:15)

The Scriptures could not be any clearer than this. God gave us life at the beginning while He was still forming us in the womb. As far as I am concerned the Supreme Court over-stepped its boundaries when it legalized abortion by ignoring God's Word (Roe V Wade, 1973). It could be assumed that life didn't begin until a child was actually born at that time since there was no scientific evidence suggesting otherwise. Now science has proven through DNA that life begins at conception, interesting that this is what God told us from the start. As far as the law is concerned our forefathers, in my opinion, didn't address this issue because it was beyond anyone's wildest imagination that people would want to kill their own children even before birth. The wisest decision possibly to ever come out of the Supreme Court was the decision to overturn Roe V Wade and put the abortion issue back in the hands of the states. At least this removes the guilt from the Nation as a whole and places it on the individual states. There is much discussion as to whether there should be exceptions concerning abortion, and if and when they should ever be legal.

Based on God's Word, my opinion is that all life is sacred and valuable to God, that being the case, it would come down to the decision that was made between the mother and the father of the unborn child. This would only be applicable if the mother's life was at stake. I think this situation is rare and with today's medical abilities more often than not, the child can still survive outside the mother's womb. I believe every effort should be made to preserve life at all cost. Notice I said the decision of the mother and the father. The Supreme Court said it was the mother's body to do with what she wanted, but that is not true. The child is a separate human being with rights the same as all other American citizens and this child was conceived by a mother and a father, not just a mother. Now for the qualifier, the father should have a right to help make this decision provided the couple is still together. I realize that he is still the father whether they are a couple or not, but it isn't his life that is at stake. If they are still a couple then he will care more about her life and the life of their child than he does his own; and therefore this decision should be made as a couple (Genesis 2:24). I do feel as though I should add here that according to God's Word the order of priority in the family unit should be God first, then the spouse, then the children and then others. With that being said; if a man chooses his child over his spouse it should only be because the two of them made that choice together. If they are a couple, then God sees them as one. If the husband's priorities are arranged according to God's Word, then the life of the mother should take precedence over the life of the child. The Bible uses the term wife, but marriages back then did not require a ceremony, a license or governmental approval (Gen 24:67). A marriage is a commitment not a governmentally approved contract. Today a marriage should consist of a monogamous commitment, a legal contract and some sort of testimonial in front of God and witnesses.

Any presidential candidate that does not have an active pro-life agenda is not worthy of the Christian vote. With the recent exposure of the horrendous practices being carried out by Planned Parenthood and the selling of baby parts for profit, this agenda should begin with the de-funding of this agency. America must stop killing innocent children. The candidate's ultimate goal should be to stop the slaughtering of innocent children in all of the states. By the way, this issue alone eliminates every possible candidate that speaks in favor of abortion regardless of their political Party affiliation. I will not name the Party, but one of the most active Parties today prides itself in promoting abortion rights without limits.

They call it removing all legal restrictions to women's health. From a Biblical view, this has little to do with women's health and everything to do with murder. Women do not have to have an abortion to be healthy in most cases. I am not suggesting that everyone in this Party is evil, but on this issue you would be hard-pressed to find anyone in this Party that would promote the rights of the unborn child. Why do I think this is the case? It is simple; the majority of the women in our country have been convinced that this is about their bodies and their health and no one else should have any say so about it. Therefore to take a stand against unborn babies is to win the largest amount of votes from women. They have turned it into a women's rights issue when that has nothing to do with it. I can recall Hillary Clinton attacking pro-life people saying this is a war on women. This has nothing to do with women's health as she would have you believe. This is about children's health. There are plenty of other women's health organizations that do not perform abortions. No one is against women's health, it is ridiculous to even suggest it, what possible reason could anyone have for wanting our women to be unhealthy? Besides, wasn't Obama care supposed to solve all of our health care problems anyway? Look at these statistics concerning abortion:

ABORTIONS IN AMERICA

INCIDENTS OF ABORTION

- A total of 730,322 abortions were reported to Centers for Disease Control for 2011, the most recent year numbers are available. (Reporting is voluntary and not 100%.)

- In 2011, the total number of abortions decreased by 5% over 2010 numbers.

- The Associated Press reported in June, 2015, that nationwide the number of abortions decreased by an average 12% since 2010.
- CDC showed that 3,932,181 babies were born in the U.S. in 2013.
- In the United States, about half of all pregnancies are unintended.
- Of all unintended pregnancies, 4 in 10 are aborted.
- Twenty-one percent of all pregnancies in the U.S. end in abortion (not including natural miscarriages).
- There has been a steady decline in abortions since 1980.
- Each year, about 1.7% of all women aged 15-44 have an abortion.
- Of the women obtaining abortions in any given year, about half of them have had at least one previous abortion.
- By age 45, one third of American women will have had at least one abortion.
- The U.S. abortion rate in 2011 was 13.9 abortions per 1,000, down from 19.4 per 1,000 in 2008.
- 88.7% of all abortions take place by the twelfth week of pregnancy.

WHY WOMEN GET ABORTION

- Some 1.06 million abortions were performed in 2011, down from 1.21 million abortions in 2008, a decline of 13%.
- Women who have never been married account for one-third of abortions in America.
- Less than 1% of all abortions take place because of rape and/or incest.

Women give an average of 3.7 reasons why they are seeking an abortion including the following:

- 21% Inadequate finances
- 21% Not ready for responsibility
- 16% Woman's life would be changed too much
- 12% Problems with relationships, unmarried
- 11% Too young and/or immature
- 8% Children are grown; she has all she wants
- 3% Baby has possible health problems
- <1% Pregnancy caused by rape/incest
- 4% Other

ABORTION BY RACE

- Blacks comprise only 13% of the population of America but account for 37% of all abortions.
- Black women are five times more likely to abort than white women.

- 69% of pregnancies among Blacks are unintended, while that number is 54% among Hispanics and 40% of pregnancies among Whites.
- Planned Parenthood, the largest seller of abortions in the United States, has located 80% of its abortion clinics in minority neighborhoods, disproportionally targeting minorities for abortion.

PUBLIC OPINION ABOUT ABORTION

Since the election of President Barack Obama, Americans have experienced a shift in how they view abortion. In the spring of 2009, several polls showed that for the first time, the majority of Americans identify themselves as "pro-life."

Not only that, those who identify themselves as "pro-choice" fell dramatically in the same time period that pro-life sentiment rose.[1]

President Biden is just another copy of President Obama. He simply strives to take the country down the same path that President Obama started down. Our next President has to be one that will stop the killing. At the very least he should de-fund Planned Parenthood. Then, if possible, take the steps needed to ensure the Supreme Court ruling concerning Roe verses Wade stays as is or abortion becomes illegal altogether accept when the mother's life is at stake. He should declare and unborn child, as of the time of conception, is a human life with all the same rights to exist as any other person. On one hand they violate

---

[1] Sources: www.census.gov, www.guttmacher.org, www.foxnews.com.

God's law to award civil rights to the LBGTQ community; on the other hand they violate God's law to take civil rights away from an unborn child, ironic.

CHRISTIAN VIEW ON IN VITRO FERTILIZATION

On February 16th 2024 the Alabama State Supreme Court passed a new controversial law concerning the status of a fertilized human egg stating that this fertilized egg is a child and not just a blob of cells as the abortion rights supporters suggest. The intent of this ruling was to preserve the life of the unborn fetus which would correspond with the overturning of Roe vs. Wade by the United States Supreme court. In other words, the intent was to preserve life in contrast to the ungodly practices of the typical so-called Women's Reproductive Health Rights crowd. As one of the results of this ruling several of the In Vitro Fertilization (IVF) clinics located in that state decided to close their doors in response citing the fear of prosecution for some of their common practices. The abortion rights activist used this as an opportunity to suggest that the over-turn of Roe vs. Wade was a bad ruling that should be reversed because these people were now subject to criminal charges for trying to help women who could not become mothers without the services provided by these clinics. The reason for this fear is because during the process of this procedure the woman's egg is fertilized in a laboratory and when this is done normally more than one egg will become fertilized at the same time. This increases the possibility of producing at least one egg that can be successfully fertilized and then placed in the mother's womb to continue to develop to maturity. The remaining fertilized eggs are then sometimes frozen and preserved for future use. Sometimes these extra eggs are discarded once it has been determined they are no longer viable or will never be used. Because of this practice these clinics supposedly feared that this ruling would subject them to prosecution due to this practice.

I believe as a Christian that all life should be considered sacred and that life does begin at conception (when the egg is fertilized). That being said, I also believe that God expects us to use a little bit of common sense along with moral principles when dealing with such sensitive issues. The fact is things always get more complicated when people get involved in events that normally occur naturally whether the involvement is meant for good or evil. If that is true then we must include the intent of the people who participated in the event and determine if it was intended for good or evil. In this case the good would be the creation of life and the evil being the destruction of life. The average person will tell you that it is God that gives life and that is true, but God also gave the mother and the father the ability and the authority to create life.

> Likewise, ye husbands, dwell with them according to knowledge, giving honour unto the wife, as unto the weaker vessel, and as being heirs together of the grace of life; that your prayers be not hindered. (1Pet 3:7)

Because of this I believe it is necessary to consider the intent of the mother and father who are using this procedure in order to create a child that they would not otherwise be able to. This makes it clear that the intent of the procedure is to create life. Even in nature itself it is a well known fact that the human body will discard any fetus that is no longer viable whatever the reason may be. Therefore I think the Christian should be in favor of the creation and preservation of life by whatever means available including IVF because the intent is to create life not to destroy it. Those who would use this controversy to support the right to destroy life by abortion clearly do not understand the significance of morality and intent. I believe that this was the intent of the Alabama Supreme Court ruling as well and that is why this has immediately resulted in additional laws being introduced for clarification. I believe the misinterpretation of this ruling was done intentionally in order to cause unrest in the general public and to stir up support for their unrighteous pursuits against the preservation of life.

CHAPTER FIVE
DEMOCRATIC SOCIALISM

WHAT IS DEMOCRATIC SOCIALISM?

Democratic Socialism is defined as a left wing political philosophy that supports political democracy and some form of socially owned economy. That sounds great in theory, but the problem is the fact that our Capitalistic economy is the only thing that separates us from a socialistic society. There are three steps that have to be taken to convert a Democratic society into a socialistic society. The first is to hire as many people to work for the government as you possibly can. (Undermine Capitalism) Second, Get as many people in the country dependent on government support as you are physically able to. (Create Government dependency) Third, take the guns away from the people so they cannot rebel. (The right to bear arms was created to prevent Governmental control) Does this sound familiar to you? Another word for income equality is socialism.

> Whatever you do, work heartily, as for the Lord and not for men. (Col 3:23)

> For even when we were with you, we would give you this command: If anyone is not willing to work, let him not eat (2 Thess 3:10)

> In all toil there is profit, but mere talk tends only to poverty. (Pr 14:23)

> A slack hand causes poverty, but the hand of the diligent makes rich. (Pr 10:4)
>
> Whoever works his land will have plenty of bread, but he who follows worthless pursuits lacks sense. (Pr 12:11)
>
> The desire of the sluggard kills him, For his hands refuse to labor. (Pr 21:25)
>
> The soul of the sluggard craves and gets nothing, while the soul of the diligent is richly supplied. (Pr 13:4)

The Scriptures are completely full of passages that refer to this topic. God made it crystal clear that if a man (meaning mankind) is willing and able to work God will surely bless him. But if he is not willing to work he will not have the things that he desires, or even requires to survive. There are also many verses that talk about giving to others and helping others, but it says to give willingly, that doesn't mean we should allow the government to take it from us to give it to someone else that doesn't deserve it. I am not suggesting that everyone that is on food stamps, or welfare, or unemployment or any other government support program is not worthy of receiving it because they won't work, but everyone knows that the system is extremely abused and many that are on these programs are on them because they just don't want to go to work. I have heard many say, "Why should I go to work when the government is paying me to stay home". There is also another word used for working hard and being rewarded for your labor, it is "Capitalism". Following is a quote from Heritage.org research:

"The nation's long-term spending trajectory remains on a fiscal collision course. Social Security, Medicare, Medicaid, and Obamacare are too large and growing rapidly. While the Budget Control Act of 2011 and sequestration are modestly restraining the discretionary budget, mandatory spending—including entitlements—continues to grow nearly unabated. Eighty-five percent of the projected growth in spending over the next decade is due to entitlement spending and interest on the debt. Obamacare is the largest driver of increasing federal health care spending, and it alone will add $1.8 trillion in federal spending by 2024."

Obama Care, or the Affordable Care Act (ACA) is the single largest tax increase in the history of our country, even though that isn't what they call it. This is the closest thing to social medicine that Obama could get to pass through congress. Social medicine is another way of saying we should take money away from the people who work to provide health care for those who won't. Obama called this another step towards income equality, but it is actually another step toward socialism. Obama Care should be repealed and another health care system put in to place that takes advantage of private companies and capitalistic competition. This is what drives cost down for the people. The government has never been able to do anything cheaper than private businesses and when the government is in control there is no competition driving costs down for the consumer. The ACA is still active today, but the worst part of the act, "the individual Mandate" has been abolished since 2019. Currently the full reinstatement of the ACA including the "the Individual Mandate" are in the hands of the Supreme Court and should President Biden be able to influence the Court towards his socialistic agendas the ACA could be fully re-established. We must elect someone who will find a way to create jobs and cut entitlements, someone who will make capitalistic policies not socialistic ones. We need someone who will get government spending back under control. Someone who will end social programs such as Obama Care and put healthcare back in the hands of private businesses. These are the policies that made our nation different and successful and they are the policies that will keep America great.

CHAPTER SIX
SAME SEX MARRIAGE

GAY RIGHTS (SAME SEX MARRIAGE)

Thou shalt not lie with mankind, as with womankind: it is an abomination. (Lev 18:22)

If a man also lie with mankind, as he lieth with a woman, both of them have committed an abomination. (Lev 20:13)

Know ye not that the unrighteous shall not inherit the kingdom of God? Be not deceived: neither fornicators, nor idolaters, nor adulterers, nor effeminate, nor abusers of themselves with mankind...... (I Cor 6:9 & 11)

Wherefore God also gave them up to uncleanness through the lust of their own hearts, to dishonour their own bodies between themselves: Who changed the truth of God into a lie, and worshiped and served the creature more that the creator, who is blessed forever. Amen. For this cause God gave them up unto vile affections: for even their women did change the natural use into that which is against nature: And likewise also the men, leaving the natural use of the woman, burned in their lust one toward another; men with men working that which is unseemly, and receiving in themselves that recompence of their error which was meet. And even as they did not like to retain God in their knowledge, God gave them over to a reprobate mind, to do those things which are not convenient. (Rom 1:24-27)

Therefore shall a man leave his father and his mother, and shall cleave unto his wife: and they shall be one flesh. And they were both naked, the man and his wife, and were not ashamed. (Gen 3:24-25)

HOW SHOULD A CHRISTIAN VOTE CONCERNING THE LGBTQ COMMUNITY

As a Christian, how do you ignore all of these Old and New Testament verses and somehow decide that there should be legislation passed that says same sex marriage should be considered a civil right? The only possible explanation is that you have determined that man's rights should over rule God's laws. I'm sorry if this offends anyone, but I am not the one who wrote those Words, they came straight from God. Today the media and the groups that promote this sinful behavior have put it all in a nice neat little package so it doesn't sound as bad as it is. They call themselves the LBGTQ community. Do you know what these letters stand for? L- Lesbian ("For this cause God gave them up unto vile affections: for even their women did change the natural use into that which is against nature:") B- Bisexual ("And likewise also the men, leaving the natural use of the woman, burned in their lust one toward another; men with men working that which is unseemly,") G- Gay (men with men and women with women) T-Transgender (Those who believe God made a mistake and equipped their bodies with the wrong genitalia) Q-Queer (relating to a sexual identity that does not correspond to established ideas of sexuality and gender, especially heterosexual based on God's Words "One man and One woman") If you believe in the God Jehovah and His Son Jesus then you cannot believe that a perfect all knowing, all powerful, Omnipresent God, creator of the heavens and the earth is capable of making these kinds of mistakes and creating people with the wrong genitalia. My God does not make mistakes.

This is not a mistake or a choice or an acceptable alternative lifestyle. It is simply sin and it is abhorrent in the eyes of God. There are many other verses that refer to this crime of men with men and women with women and the fact that it is an abomination to God, but I think you get the point. The word abomination means, atrocity, disgrace, horror, obscenity, outrage, crime, evil, monstrosity. The Supreme Court struck again when they turned Obama's Nation into an abomination. This is the clear result of worshiping the creature more than the creator just as God said. In modern terms that means placing man's laws over God's laws, or civil rights over God given rights. I am not trying to attack the LBGTQ community. I am simply pointing out the fact that to God these types of relationships are sin. I know it is difficult to love someone and not be allowed to express that love because of man's laws or God's laws. In either case to ignore the laws of man is to break the laws of God because God is the one who puts governments and legal systems in places of authority. Therefore to break man's laws is the same as breaking God's laws. Even though, in the United States right now, our government has chosen to ignore God's laws and legalize these relationships, but that doesn't change God's opinion on the matter. I believe anyone who is willing to walk away from someone they love in order please God is someone with strong faith. This is what is necessary to keep a good relationship with God because these relationships are sinful and you cannot be forgiven by God for a sin that you are not willing to give up. I believe that by passing these laws that our nation has scarred its relationship with God and in order to correct this mistake the nation must also repent and change course on this decision. If God's people want to bring back God's blessings on America we must try to bring America back to God.

THE CRIMINALIZATION OF CHRISTIANITY

One of our 2016 Presidential candidates worded it in yet another way, Mike Huckabee said:

> "I visited Kim Davis in the Carter County Detention Center this afternoon and had the honor of walking out with her as she was released.
>
> When I warned that the Supreme Court's decision on marriage would lead to the criminalization of Christianity in America I was dismissed by many as an alarmist and

my comments were mocked by the chattering class. Now, just two months after the court's lawless ruling, an elected county clerk was put in jail by an unelected judge for refusing to issue a "marriage" license to a same-sex couple, removing all doubts about criminalization of Christianity in this country.

This threat to our faith is real and we need a President who understands this. I will fight for Religious Liberty and reject judicial tyranny"

This is one of the reasons that I believe God wants me to write this book, because the majority of the people I talk to, even Christians, have no idea what is going on in our country. In actuality, I am not judging the person committing these crimes or even the act itself, I am only reminding the people of our nation of what God said about it. It surprises me that many people, again even Christians, are fooled into accepting this crime as an acceptable alternative lifestyle in the name of human rights. God created man with a free will and they are free to do whatever they want, but to force the people of faith to go along with this under the penalty of the law is a clear violation of the freedom of religion.

"The **First Amendment (Amendment I)** to the United States Constitution prohibits the making of any law respecting an establishment of religion, impeding the free exercise of religion, abridging the freedom of speech, infringing on the freedom of the press, interfering with the right to peaceably assemble or prohibiting the petitioning for a governmental redress of grievances. It was adopted on December 15, 1791, as one of the ten amendments that constitute the Bill of Rights."

On Friday, June 26, 2015 the Supreme Court ruled 5-4 to redefine marriage across the nation to include same-sex unions. Justice Antonin Scalia was one of the dissenting justices. Following are some of his most significant dissents:

> "The Federal Judiciary is hardly a cross-section of America. Take, for example, this Court, which consists of only nine men and women, all of them successful lawyers who studied at Harvard or Yale Law School. Four of the nine are natives of New York City. Eight of them grew up in east- and west-coast States. Only one hails from the vast expanse in-between. Not a single South-westerner or even, to tell the truth, a genuine Westerner (California does not count). Not a single evangelical Christian (a group that comprises about one quarter of Americans), or even a Protestant of any denomination... to allow the policy question of same-sex marriage to be considered and resolved by a select, patrician, highly unrepresentative panel of nine is to violate a principle even more fundamental than no

taxation without representation: no social transformation without representation."

"The opinion is couched in a style that is as pretentious as its content is egotistic. . . 'The nature of marriage is that, through its enduring bond, two persons together can find other freedoms, such as expression, intimacy, and spirituality.' (Really? Who ever thought that intimacy and spirituality [whatever that means] were freedoms? And if intimacy is, one would think Freedom of Intimacy is abridged rather than expanded by marriage. Ask the nearest hippie. Expression, sure enough, is a freedom, but anyone in a long-lasting marriage will attest that that happy state constricts, rather than expands, what one can prudently say.)"

"If, even as the price to be paid for a fifth vote, I ever joined an opinion for the Court that began: 'The Constitution promises liberty to all within its reach, a liberty that includes certain specific rights that allow persons, within a lawful realm, to define and express their identity,' I would hide my head in a bag. The Supreme Court of the United States has descended from the disciplined legal reasoning of John Marshall and Joseph Story to the mystical aphorisms of the fortune cookie."

This argument began with the basic truth that according to God's Word, same sex relationships are evil and a crime. That however is not the end of it, the fact is that this decision was not only made illegally, because the Supreme Court can only interpret laws, not make them, but this as Mike Huckabee stated, opens the door to the "criminalization of Christianity" Christians are now being punished by the laws of man for practicing their faith. I believe we have to elect a candidate that not only believes that same sex marriage is wrong but also will seek a path that will reverse this decision.

CHAPTER SEVEN
TERRORISM

THE FIGHT AGAINST TERRORISM

> If you walk in My statutes and keep My commandments, and perform them... you shall eat your bread to the full, and dwell in your land safely. I will give you peace in the land, and you shall lie down, and none will make you afraid; I will rid the land of evil beasts, and the sword will not go through your land. You will chase your enemies, and they shall fall by the sword before you. Five of you shall chase a hundred, and a hundred of you shall put ten thousand to flight; your enemies shall fall by the sword before you. (Lev 26:3)

> For the Lord your God walks in the midst of your camp, to deliver you and give your enemies over to you; therefore your camp shall be holy, that He may see no unclean thing among you, and turn away from you. (Deut 23:14)

These verses reveal to us the terms that God laid down for the children of Israel in reference to keeping them safe from their enemies and preserving their land. God made it plain to them, they were to keep His commandments and walk in the ways that God wanted them to, that if they would do this He would protect them from their enemies, they would have no one to fear and they would live in peace. All of the blessings that God promised were based on the people of God keeping themselves separated from the rest of the wicked world round them and following the commandments that He had given them. If our nation will keep itself pure and separate itself from the sinfulness in the rest of the world and live by God's laws we will have the same blessings.

God's Annointing for an Offensive Approach to Battle

> Behold, I give you the authority to trample on serpents and scorpions, and over all the power of the enemy, and nothing shall by any means hurt you. (Lk 10:19)
>
> Through You we will push down our enemies; through Your name we will trample those who rise up against us. For I will not trust in my bow, nor shall my sword save me. But You have saved us from our enemies, and have put to shame those who hated us. In God we boast all day long, and praise Your name forever. (Ps 44:5)
>
> For the eyes of the Lord run to and fro throughout the whole earth, to show Himself strong on behalf of those whose heart is loyal to Him. (2Chron 16:9)

The verses pertaining to a righteous nation fighting for its' way of life and the freedom to worship God are endless, but I can't put them all here. Many would blame President Bush for starting the war on terrorism in our great nation, but it is obvious to me that on September 11th, 2001 the fight was started by the terrorist. Not only does God justify the fight, but He promises His blessings on the effort and a victory over the enemy. War is not what anybody wants, but if we as Americans want to preserve our way of life and the freedoms that we have, then we must be willing to make the necessary sacrifices. Obama knows that people hate war and he used this as an opportunity to win an election by promising to end the war. Officially he ended the war, but at what cost? I know America doesn't want to be at war, but in actuality we are still at war regardless of what Obama says. The terrorist are still at war with us. By pretending the war is over and ignoring the cries of our allies for help to finish a war that began with us is inhumane and unjustifiable. All Obama cared about is keeping campaign promises that he was never able to fulfill.

This is a war between good and evil. That is apparent by the way in which our enemies conduct themselves. Christians desire to live in a peaceful world and try not to interfere with those who do not believe the same way that we do, but the enemy will not let it go. Some politicians believe that if we leave them alone, then they will leave us alone. That is not how radical Islam works. Because we are a Nation of mostly Christians we are their sworn enemies. "Death to the infidels is their battle cry". The Christians' view is each person has the right to worship any god that they want without interference, but the radical Islamist belief is that all who don't believe the way they do should die. In America we have only suffered a few small attacks since 9/11, but in other parts of the world where we left them to fend for themselves, Christians are being slaughtered by the thousands. Am I the only one who finds it strange that we are willing to take in 200,000 Muslim refugees, but have turned our backs on persecuted Christians all over the world? Under the Biden administration these lawless people are not even required to try to seek refugee status or citizenship. Biden is simply allowing them to cross over the border and stay without any way of keeping track of who they are or how many. Every day there are thousands of illegal immigrants coming into the country and we have no way of knowing how many have terroristic intentions.

Because of Obama's retreat policies America has more blood on its' hands than at any other time in history. We had no choice but to fight back when the World Trade Center towers were attacked and frankly I had not, in my lifetime, seen more pride, patriotism or enthusiasm in the American people than was evident at that time. Today many Americans are ashamed because this is not who we are. Many of my Christian friends have stopped flying the American flag and started flying the Christian flag. When President Obama first took office Michelle Obama proclaimed, "For the first time in my life I am proud of my country", today many Americans are saying, "For the first time in my life, I'm ashamed of my country". Obama's foreign policy has been a disaster. You simply cannot draw a line in the sand against your enemy and then when they cross that line you simply ignore it. This makes America appear weak and inconsequential in the world.

To make matters worse, after that Obama turned his back on Israel and made a nuclear weapons deal with one of our worst enemies (Iran). Their leader and their people hate us and call us the Great Satan. They have promised to destroy Israel within the next 25 years and promised to come after the great Satan (America) next. Iran is the largest sponsor of terrorism in the world and America gave them 150 billion dollars to promote their tyranny. Israel's Prime minister, Benjamin Netanyahu has proclaimed that not only will this deal not prevent Iran from obtaining a nuclear weapon, but it will guarantee it. How can we do such a thing and say that we are Israel's ally? Many of the republican candidates have been very vocal about their opposition to this deal. Several Democratic congressmen and senators have also broken party lines and verbally expressed their concern. Every Republican congressman and Senator has rejected the deal along with two-thirds of the American population, but because of party loyalty this deal has been made. There is no point in crying over spilt milk and the deal is now done.

NUMBER ONE CRISIS TODAY

Today the number one crisis in the world is the war in Israel with Hamas. America's focus has been on the war between the Russians and the Ukrainians. I agree that the outcome of the war with Ukraine is important and I believe that the Ukrainians have every right to their independence from Russia, but is this more important than the fight between Israel and the Hamas,

I think not. I don't believe it was a coincidence that Hamas started this war with Israel at this particular time. They know that America cannot afford to support two wars at one time and we have already committed so much to the Ukrainians that we are further in debt than ever before in history. Biden never-the-less, intends to continue the support to Ukraine at the same level and throw a few crumbs to Israel at the same time. How long do you think this can continue? This is Hamas' best opportunity to take advantage of the current situation. We turned our back on Israel with the Iranian nuclear deal and now Biden (Obama's protégé) will turn his back on Israel again. He claims to support Israel with all we have and then he proposes a support package with 60 billion to Ukraine and 14 billion to Israel. In addition to that he has pledged his loyalty to the Democratic Party in insisting that he will not approve any additional support to Israel without additional support to the Ukraine. I truly feel for the Ukrainians and the position they are in, but America and Christians all over the world, along with the Democratic nations, should all be backing Israel first. In the current battle between Israel and the Hamas, the Israelites are being portrayed as evil doers by the world because they intend to end this war once for all with the Hamas by a ground invasion into Gaza which would result in a considerable loss of life among the civilian population. They are also being accused of war crimes due to their relentless bombing of Gaza during the preparations for their ground assault. What the world refuses to see (even President Biden) is that it is impossible for Israel to defend themselves against the Hamas with any hope of success without attacking Gaza with all the force they can. This is because Hamas has buried themselves in Gaza in their secret tunnel system and among the civilian population. They are mingling their militant forces with the general population in order to use the people as a shield. They are using hospitals and other general public places to base their operations. President Biden continues to attempt to persuade the American people that the Palestinian people are not the same as the Hamas. In America this is true, but in Gaza the Hamas has made it so that the Palestinians and the Hamas cannot be distinguished one from the other. The Israelis did not start this fight, but they will do whatever it takes to end it and America should be their strongest ally.

CHAPTER EIGHT
SUPPORTING THE MILITARY

MILITARY STRENGTH

> The LORD is my strength and song, and he is become my salvation: he is my God, and I will prepare him an habitation; my father's God, and I will exalt him. The LORD is a man of war: the LORD is his name. (Ex 15:2-3)

> And when the Lord thy God shall delivers them before thee; thou shalt smite them, and utterly destroy them; thou shalt make no covenant with them, nor show mercy unto them: neither shalt thou make marriages with them; thy daughter thou shalt not unto his son, nor his daughter shalt thou take unto thy son. For they will turn away thy son from following me, that they may serve other gods: so will the anger of the LORD be kindled against you, and destroy thee suddenly. (Deut 7:2-4)

In these verses it is easy to see that God knows what is in mankind's heart. The Israelites were told that they must be willing to fight to preserve their way of life because the people in the world will not follow the one true God Jehovah. God promised to be with them in this fight, but they still had to provide the army and be ready to take the necessary actions to keep their land holy. It is plain that the reason for this was because they were to remain separate from the world and not allow themselves to be corrupted with false god's and false religions. In order to accomplish that they must maintain a strong military and be ready to fight. Now since Hamas has attacked Israel on October 7th, 2023 we are in the position where we need a strong military more than ever. We are now approaching that two war front scenario that we have feared would come. If America continues to stand behind Israel in the coming days other countries will eventually get involved and we will have no choice but to step up our role in the defense of Israel. Recently President Biden has begun showing signs of faltering under world pressure to talk Israel into a cease fire or a humanitarian pause to the assault on Gaza. Israel has insisted there will be no pause until Hamas has released all the hostages that were taken during their attack on Israel on October 7th and surrender. Will Biden stick by Israel knowing that with the military strength that remains after the Obama down sizing and Biden's own weakening of the military with his Covid 19 mandatory vaccine policy that forced 1700 sailors from the Navy alone out of the military.

If we take such a stand then it goes without saying that America must have a strong military presence in the world. "World peace through world strength has always been a much stronger deterrent to war than mere negotiations and false deal making. Everyone knows Iran will not keep a deal with America as they have broken every deal in the past. The one thing that we learn from history is the fact that we never learn anything from history. We should have known ever since Obama took office that he was going to put us in this sort of position. One of the things that he continually strove to do during his administration was to cut our military. It is important to see what the policy of Obama was during his administration because they are representative of the Democratic Party and of President Biden who was President Obama's puppet. Following is a portion of an article from the Washington Times:

U.S. MILITARY DECIMATED IUNDER OBAMA, ONLY 'MARGINALLY ABLE' TO DEFEND NATION

The *U.S. military* is shedding so many troops and weapons it is only "marginally able" to defend the nation and falls short of the Obama administration's national security strategy, according to a new report by The Heritage Foundation on Tuesday.

"The *U.S. military* itself is aging. It's shrinking in size," said *Dakota Wood*, a Heritage analyst. "And it's quickly becoming problematic in terms of being able to address more than one major conflict."

President Obama's latest strategy is to size the armed forces so that the four military branches have sufficient troops, ships, tanks and aircraft to win a large war, while simultaneously acting to "deny the objectives of — or impose unacceptable costs on — another aggressor in another region."

> In other words, the Quadrennial Defense Review says the *military* can essentially fight two major conflicts at once. It could defeat an invasion of South Korea by the North, for example, and stop Russia from invading Western Europe or Iran from conquering a Persian Gulf state.
>
> But Heritage's "2015 Index of *U.S. Military* Strength" took a look, in detail, at units and weapons, region by region, and came to a different conclusion. [2]

For more details concerning the cuts to the military under Obama please read the remainder of this article that is referenced in the foot note.

Despite the damage that Obama has caused to our military we are still a dominant force in the realm of world powers, but it seems as though he wanted us to be weak and unable to defend ourselves. President Trump was able to at least temporarily eliminate the threat of terrorism in America for now, but with President Biden's disastrous border dilemma in play it is only a matter of time until the terrorist will strategically develop strong holds on American soil and the terrorism will be here as prevalent as it is in other countries with open borders. With Biden's additional policies concerning the mandated Covid vaccines and his woke policy campaign which has the military spending its time and resources training Airforce cadets to avoid using "microagressions" by

---

[2] By Rowan Scarborough - The Washington Times - Tuesday, February 24, 2015

replacing terms such as "you guys", "terrorist" and "Mom and Dad" with terms that are considered "less offensive", followed by continual lectures on race and gender identity pronouns. We must elect someone who is willing to fight the war on terrorism, do whatever has to be done to stop Iran from becoming a nuclear power, preserve Democratic societies throughout the world such as Ukraine, defend other countries and ourselves from bullies in the world like Russia and defend our allies like Israel from radicals such as the Hamas, while we still have the ability to do so. Will President Biden keep his word and stick by Israel even after the pressure being put on him by the American citizens, random Rabis, the Palestinian supporters and their European allies after Obama's weakening of the military and the damage that Biden has caused with his own damaging policies? I guess we will just have to wait and see.

CHAPTER NINE
ILLEGAL IMMIGRATION

OPEN BORDERS

> Thou shalt not remove thy neighbor's landmark, which they of old time have set, in thine inheritance which thou shalt inherit, in the land that Jehovah thy God giveth thee to possess it. (Deut 19:14)

> Remove not thy ancient landmark, which thy fathers have set. (Pr 22:28)

> And the border shall go down to the Jordan, and the goings out thereof shall be at the Salt Sea. This shall be your land according to the borders thereof round about. (Num 34:12)

> And as for the western border, ye shall have even the great sea for a border; this shall be your west border. (Num 34:6)

> When the Most High gave the nations their inheritance, When He separated the sons of man, He set the boundaries of the peoples According to the number of the sons of Israel. (Deut 32: 8)

In the Old Testament, borders were significant and meaningful to the Israelites as God's people and today in America, we who are Christians, are also God's people. We must understand that in order to maintain a Christian based society, which is what our nation was founded on, we must control who and how many people are allowed to immigrate legally into our country. The problem with open borders which results in illegal immigration is that it is impossible to even know who is crossing into our country much less how many. This is the reason for establishing and maintaining borders. It is not for the purpose of discrimination, but rather the purpose of preservation.

WHO IS TASKED WITH BORDER SECURITY?

Let every soul be subject unto the higher powers. For there is no power but of God: the powers that be are ordained of God. Whosoever therefore resisteth the power, resisteth the ordinance of God: and they that resist shall receive to themselves damnation. For rulers are not a terror to good works, but to the evil. Will thou then not be afraid of the power? do that which is good, and thou shalt have praise of the same: For he is the minister of God to thee for good. But if thou do that which is evil, be afraid; for he beareth not the sword in vain: for he is the minister of God, a revenger to execute wrath upon him that doeth evil. Wherefore ye must needs be subject, not only for wrath, but also for conscience sake. For this cause pay ye tribute also: for they are God's ministers, attending continually upon this very thing. Render therefore to all their dues: tribute to whom tribute is due; custom to whom custom; fear to whom fear; honour to whom honour. (Rom 13:1-7)

In those verses the Apostle Paul makes it very clear that not only are we supposed to listen to the officials placed over us, but they are ministers of God placed in these positions of authority in order to maintain order and punish those who break the law. It is therefore obvious then that our government is responsible for establishing and maintaining borders and border enforcement laws.

THE CONSEQUENCES OF ILLEGAL IMMIGRATION

In 2007, 12 million immigrants remained illegally in the US. Today there is an estimated 11.4 million illegal immigrants living in the United States. In the fiscal year of 2022 the number of illegal immigrants entering the U. S. topped 2.76 million and now in the fiscal year 2023 the CBP (Customs and Border Patrol) just released the numbers for this year as 3.2 million breaking all previous records. This is an increase of 16 percent over 2022 and a 63 % increase over 2021. This one year under President Biden illegal immigration has increased more than all four years with President Trump combined. God never tells us to turn down immigrants or to be cruel to them in any way. The question here is not about immigrants, it is about them entering the country illegally. Today the population in America increases each year more by the number of illegal immigrants than by those born here as natural citizens. So what are the consequences of out of control immigration?

Out of control costs in education: In 1982 a Supreme Court ruling forced local schools to provide education for illegal's. With the addition of each student it adds $10,000 in costs. This one ruling alone costs Alabama $482 million.

The Rise in Crime and overcrowded prisons: Today one quarter of all those in American prisons is an illegal alien. For every dozen of illegal immigrants, one of them already has a criminal background. Some of our most violent gangs and international crime syndicates have come here through illegal immigration as well as the overwhelming majority of illegal drugs and human trafficking.

The overwhelming of the budgets of the States for healthcare and for the homeless. The Congressional Budget Office says that each illegal family takes out of the economy $89,000 more than they contribute. The Tennessee Health Care system spends $15 billion a year on emergency room care for illegals. I find it ironic how all the States that consider themselves sanctuary States are now screaming about being overwhelmed when they were fine with illegal immigration until Governor Greg Abbott of Texas started sending the problem to their door step.

Substantial increase in the national terror threat: The CBP recently released year end data that reveals the apprehension of a record 172 individuals that are on the terror watch list trying to cross the border illegally in 2023. In the mean time President Biden just submitted a request of 13.6 billion dollars to fund his open-border policies that have only created havoc on American cities and increased the terrorism threat in America substantially. [3]

WHO IS TO BLAME?

We could go on about illegal immigration without end, but I believe I have sufficiently represented the problem. I do feel that it is important to make it clear that for the most part, the fault for this dilemma is not on the immigrants themselves. You cannot blame people from other nations for seeking out a better life for themselves and their families. Speaking for myself, and I believe most Christians would agree, it is not immigration that is the problem. The problem is illegal immigration and President Biden's Open-Border policy that has turned this border situation into a significant threat to our country and our way of life. The Bible teaches that we are to treat immigrants the same way we would anyone else so long as they have entered the country legally. If they have entered the country illegally then they should be treated as criminals because that is what illegally means.

> And if a stranger sojourn with thee in your land, ye shall not vex him. But the stranger that dwelleth with you shall be unto you as one born among you, and thou shalt

---

[3] The Federation For American Immigration Reform, Latest Immigration News, October 25th, 2023

> love him as thyself; for ye were strangers in the land of Egypt: I am the LORD your God. (Lev 19:33-34)

Those who are referred to as sojourners or foreigners were considered temporary residents, but not citizens of Israel. They were expected to keep all the same laws as the Israeli people were, but they were not afforded all the same privileges as Israeli citizens were. (Deut 16:9-15)

There are examples in the Bible were the rise in status of the strangers, or the immigrants to the point that they were elevated above the Israelites was a result of Israel's disobedience and was a punishment from God. If America continues down this current path of disobedience to God's Word and continues this policy of open-borders then perhaps this will be our punishment as well.

> The stranger that is within thee shall get up above thee very high; and thou shalt come down very low. He shall lend to thee, and thou shalt not lend to him: he shall be the head and thou shalt be the tail. Moreover all these curses shall come upon thee, and shall pursue thee, and overtake thee, till thou be destroyed; because thou hearkenedst not unto the voice of the LORD thy God, to keep his commandments and his statutes which he commanded thee: (Deut 28:43-45)

ILLEGAL IMMIGRATION IS STILL ILLEGAL

The role of the individual Christian is to show mercy, but the role of the civil authority is to execute justice. As believers, we are to display the love of Christ to everyone, legal or illegal. But the role of the government is to defend citizens against law-breaking activity such as illegal immigration.

There have been a number of different approaches to the immigration problem by numerous past presidents ranging from building a wall and suggesting that the Mexican Government pay for it, to rounding up all the illegal immigrants and sending them back to Mexico or where-ever they may have come from. America has the most generous immigration policies in the world. The problem is illegal entry and those who stay past their legal status time. The immigrants who come here legally, for the most part, are law abiding citizens whom have made great sacrifices to come here and have made significant contributions to our society. President Obama and President Biden have contributed to this problem by ignoring the illegal immigration laws that are already on the books and refusing to pass any new laws dealing with the problem. The border patrol has been told to allow them in and has refused to deport those that have been caught even when they have committed serious crimes. Government has also refused to make the States enforce current immigration laws and thus the development of so-called sanctuary cities. We need a candidate who will take a common sense practical approach in stopping the illegal immigration and dealing with the illegal immigrants that are already here, in particularly those who are convicted criminals. He needs to be a candidate who will enforce the law and require the States to do the same. Simply putting a stop to sanctuary cities would be a good place to start. We need to end this irrational policy of allowing laws to be broken or changed in the name of civil rights. This is just another form of lawlessness that seems to be affecting every part of our society.

Chapter Ten
The National Debt

The National Debt must be repaid

It has been said that the national debt is irrelevant and just a number that has no meaning because the United States will never repay it and this is understood by the entire world. For a Christian however, debt is a real problem for our country and it must be repaid.

> Better not to vow than to vow and not pay. (Eccl 5:5)

Considering this Biblical principal there are several problems concerning debt that must be dealt with. If this debt must be repaid, but all we do is continue to push the cart down the road, it will be our children that will eventually suffer the consequences. We cannot count on things getting better in the future. We cannot continue to sacrifice the future of our children on the altar of our present greed.

> Come now, you who say, 'Today or tomorrow we will go to such and such a city, spend a year there, buy and sell, and make a profit; whereas you do not know what will happen tomorrow. For what is your life? It is even a vapor that appears for a little time and then vanishes away. (Jms 4:13-14)

> A good man leaves an inheritance to his children's children, but the wealth of the sinner is stored up for the righteous. (Pr 13:22)

> But if anyone does not provide for his own, and especially for those of his household, he has denied the faith and is worse than an unbeliever. (1 Tim 5:8)

Debt results in the enslavement of the borrower by the lender.

> The rich rules over the poor, and the borrower is servant to the lender. (Pr 22:7)

It surprises me how little people seem to care about debt these days. Every day I have debt relief organizations calling me wanting to know if I am interested in getting out of the debt that I owe. Everyone is looking for a get rich quick scheme or they are trying to find ways to get out of paying the debt that they have made. According to God's Word failure to repay your debt is considered stealing.

> The wicked borrows and does not repay,
> But the righteous shows mercy and gives.
> (Ps 37:21)

> If a man makes a vow to the Lord, or swears an oath to bind himself by some agreement, he shall not break his word; he shall do according to all that proceeds out of his mouth. (Num 30:2)

The Bible says if we can't be trusted with the things that God has given us on earth as stewards, then how can we expect to blessed with the riches of heaven.

> He who is faithful in what is least is faithful also in much; and he who is unjust

> in what is least is unjust also in much. Therefore, if you have not been faithful in the unrighteous mammon, who will commit to your trust the true riches? And if you have not been faithful in what is another man's, who will give you what is your own. (Lk 16:10-12)

If America continues to borrow at our current pace it will not be long until everything we have will belong to China or other nations because of the inability to pay back our debt. America is the greatest nation in the world; great nations have been brought to destruction by overwhelming debt. The foreigner will grow to be mightier than the lender.

> The alien who is among you shall rise higher and higher above you, and you shall come down lower and lower. He shall lend to you, but you shall not lend to him; he shall be the head, and you shall be the tail. Moreover, all these curses shall come upon you and pursue and overtake you, until you are destroyed, because you did not obey the voice of the Lord your God, to keep His commandments and His statues which He commanded you. (Deut 28: 43-45)

GOING IN DEEPER AND DEEPER

It is a fact that the national debt is turning into another type of crisis. The debt has been blown up by both parties and by the majority of the presidents. This trend has to stop. It is a fact that the national debt was doubled under President Bush, but it is also true that it was tripled under President Obama. Then the national debt increased by 7.8 trillion during Trump's presidency to 27.75 trillion. As of July 14, 2023 and then just a little more than halfway through President Biden's term the debt had risen to 32.5 trillion and today it is now more than 33 trillion.

We need a President that will make sure we pass a budget that will eventually lead to our Nation being debt free. I realize this can no longer happen in just one or two terms under anyone, Democrat or Republican, but we need to at least start heading in the right direction. We cannot press forward with business as usual and borrowing money for future generations to deal with. Like the Bible says, borrowing and not paying back is stealing. If I understand correctly what I have heard, this was part of the issue with the Republican Party and the expulsion of the House Speaker Kevin McCarthy by the far right members of the House. These far right members were trying to convince the Party that we could not continue down the road of uncontrolled spending for anybody in need. Of course for making such suggestions they were ridiculed by the left and the media.

CHAPTER ELEVEN
STOP LAWLESSNESS

LAW ENFORCEMBENT

I do not need to list more Scripture for this topic, everyone knows that violence against the police, destruction of other people's property for no reason and murdering police officers is morally wrong and illegal. The Democratic Party's snuggling up to the Black Lives Matter group can only be explained by the fact that they are trying to win votes. We all know black lives matter as do all lives and we understand that they are trying to emphasize that blacks are being killed by police in large numbers and it needs to stop. However, when they are asked about what they want to do about the problem they have no answer. I heard mass incarceration has to stop. Here we go again with; we now want to stop crime in America by making everything criminals do legal. The number of people doing a certain thing should have no bearing on its moral or legal status. If you don't want to go to jail don't commit a crime. There have been a number of times in my life when I have been treated poorly and even unfairly by the police and lawyers. Often-times when people are arrested, even if they are innocent, they are treated like they are guilty by the arresting agents. In America we are supposed to be innocent until proven guilty and it seems like much of the time people who are arrested are treated as guilty until proven innocent and sometimes even after that. Some of that may be due to the position of authority going to the head of the arresting agent, but it may also be because even though a person may be totally innocent the officer of the law has no way of knowing that. If they were to treat you as an innocent person and you were not, then you would have the upper hand. In order to have a peaceful society we must have laws and we must respect and support those who enforce them. I would not want to be a police officer in the world we live in today.

MIKE HUCKABEE ON LAWLESSNESS

"On the heels of their summer convention, Democratic leaders passed a resolution to support the Black Lives Matters movement and condemn American police officers. The very next day, movement protesters marched in Minnesota, chanting death threats against police, shouting "pigs in a blanket, fry 'em like bacon." Dr. Martin Luther King, Jr. would be appalled by such violent and intemperate language, and Americans should be appalled by the Democrat Party's support for the Black Lives Matter mob.

From Baltimore to Beverly Hills, this movement has incited violence, chaos and disrespect. It's time for President Obama and the Democrat Party to stop pandering to a movement that riots and supports violence against police. How many law enforcement deaths will it take for the political class to stand with the people who put their lives on the line to keep us safe?

A very small minority of police officers certainly abuse their power, and when they do, they should be punished accordingly. But most police officers are overworked and underpaid public servants, and take risks that most of us would run from. These heroes are the thin blue line that separates our safety from total anarchy.

When I was governor, I carried out the death sentence of 16 criminals, more than any other governor in our state's history. These were the most difficult decisions I have made in my life, but I had months to pour over all the evidence, ask questions, and carefully deliberate. I had the luxury of time to review each case with meticulous precision.

When a police officer knocks on a front door late-at-night or approaches a vehicle on the side of a dirt road, they have no idea what to expect or anticipate. They make split-second decisions. Most often, these encounters are uneventful. But in the face of real danger, an officer who fails to respond quickly or decisively may never see his or her family again. The stakes are high. Law enforcement officers deserve our appreciation and admiration—not our condemnation.

President Obama assumed office and I genuinely hoped he would use his presidency to unify America. But under his watch, racial riots and rampages have only grown worse. Black lives matter because ALL lives matter. Haven't we learned from history? It would be very helpful for our President to state the obvious.

From the child in the womb to the dying adult in a hospital bed, life has intrinsic value. Whether black, white, brown, young or old, ALL lives matter. It's time we stop burning cars, shooting cops, and recognize that life is a gift from God.

I grew up with holes in my shoes attending grade school with children that had much more than me. My mother taught me that no one was better than me, but I wasn't better than anyone else.

I was raised in the segregated south. I have seen the "whites only" water fountains with my own eyes. Racism is a wound that runs deep in our country, and it's a shameful stain on our history. Racism exists because we have a sin problem in America, not a skin problem. It's the result of the sin of pride believing oneself to be better than another.

As a country, we have witnessed fire-hosings, whippings, boycotts, marches and martyrs. Dr. King himself was assassinated.

> He died, but his dream didn't. Others were killed and their deaths never earned a news headline.
>
> And when you elevate the life or death of anyone because of their race, you demean and diminish all those who shed blood to overcome racism."[4]

It is my opinion that the majority of these issues all stem from one thing **LAWLESSNESS**. This lawlessness is prevalent from the White-house to the Court House to the Jail house. We must elect a president that will enforce the current laws and oversee a government and a nation that will change the laws that are no longer adequate in an effort to restore our nation's morality. We must vote for a President that will support law enforcement and the penalties that are described under the law for the violation of such laws. We need a President that will force the States to enforce Federal laws and local State laws. We should all be in this together. You cannot stop lawlessness by eliminating the laws. Order must be maintained in a civilized society and enforcing the laws is the only way to accomplish that.

---

[4] Article originally ran on DailyCaller.com.
Permalink:http://mikehuckabee.com/2015/9/the-appalling-recklessness-of-the-black-lives-matter-movement-and-the-democrat-party

CHAPTER TWELVE
THE RIGHT TO BEAR ARMS

THE FIREARM CONTROVERSY

I know this book is full of controversial topics and some even controversial among Christians of the same faith. I am not sure that I completely understand why that is true other than some either don't know what the Bible teaches about certain topics or they just simply don't care what God says. How can anyone claim to be a Christian and still believe that abortion should be a matter of choice? I believe this topic concerning the right to bear arms falls into this same category. There are many good people on both sides of the argument. My personal opinion is that if you outlaw guns, then only outlaws will have guns. If only outlaws have guns who is there to stop the lawlessness. You say the law or the police. The fact is by the time police arrive at a scene where an illegal gun has been used to commit a crime it is way too late. The crime has already taken place and the criminal is long gone. I agree wholeheartedly that there is entirely too much gun violence in America; the question is how you stop it. I don't believe taking the weapons away from law-abiding citizens is the best way to prevent criminals from using weapons. It is not guns that kill people; it is people that kill people. More specifically it is criminals that kill law-abiding citizens and one of the reasons is because many law-abiding citizens have no means to defend themselves and the criminals are aware of it. One thing that makes little sense to me is a law that allows citizens to carry a weapon, but only if they conceal it. This only results in more violence because a hidden weapon carried by a legal citizen does nothing to deter a criminal from attempting to use his illegal weapon. Never the less the answer to the problem, in my opinion, is not violating the second amendment by taking guns from law-abiding citizens, but rather taking them away from the mentally ill and the criminals. In the mean time, until we figure out how to do that, every law-abiding citizen in the country, who desires to carry a weapon, should be allowed to do so openly provided they have been properly trained and evaluated.

WHAT THE BIBLE SAYS

Since I do realize that you are not reading this material in order to find out what my opinion is, but rather what God says a Christian should do, then let's take a look at Bible references dealing with this topic. I believe Christians should always allow the Word of God to determine their position on all topics, regardless of their personal beliefs or opinions. That being the case there are a couple of things I'd like to point out scripturally. First God would remind us that it is people who are evil not things such as guns or knives. Weapons are inanimate instruments that can be used for good or evil.

> For out of the heart proceed evil thoughts, murderers, adulteries, fornications, thefts, false witness, blasphemies: (Matt 15:19)

Cain, the very first man born, out of the evilness of his heart killed his brother. Since there was no such thing as a gun back then Cain probably used a wooden club or a rock. Will we outlaw sticks and rocks? (Gen 4:8)

Second, the freedom to use self-defence illustrates the value of life. In Genesis chapter 9 God commands Noah to ensure that life is valued and protected by instituting the death penalty.

> Whoever sheddeth man's blood, by man shall his blood be shed: for in the image of God made he man. (Gen 9:6)

This was only allowed as a punishment that was intended to preserve and protect life. Which makes me want to touch on another point briefly? Those people who claim that they protest against the death penalty because they are Christians. The death penalty was instituted by God and it is through the death penalty that Christianity is even possible. You can only become a Christian by recognizing the fact that Jesus was put to death to pay for your sins. This death penalty mentioned in Genesis 9:6 is later extended to the protection of private property in Exodus 22:2

In the Book of Luke Jesus proclaimed to his disciples that the time had come for them to arm themselves for the purpose of self-defence.

> Then said he unto them, But now, he that hath a purse, let him take it, and likewise his scrip: and he that hath no sword, let him sell his garment, and buy one. (Lk 22:36)

It is a man's responsibility to provide protection for his family. Without the ability to bear arms the lawful citizens of our country would be taking a rock to a gun fight. (1 Tim 5:8) The main points of this discussion were derived from an article by William Wolfe. For more on this topic please reference the notes at the bottom of this page.[5]

To be fair, there is at least as many scriptures in the Bible that can be used to convince people that any kind of violence is wrong and God teaches us that we should turn the other cheek. For this reason I believe it is unfair to condemn anyone for their view concerning either owning their own personal weapon or not. On the other hand, if that is true then Biblically speaking, so long as a Christian obeys the laws of the land they should have the freedom to choose what is right for them.

> Therefore to him that knoweth to do good, and doeth it not, to him it is sin. (Jms 4:17)

THE SECOND AMENDMENT

The only part of this argument that remains is the argument that we have been guaranteed the right to bear arms by the Constitution of the United States and the Second Amendment. So what does the Second Amendment say in regards to the issue of the right to bear arms and why?

---

[5] God and Guns: A Biblical Worldview Analysis of the Second Amendment and Self-Defence, by William Wolfe, Friday, July 8, 2022

"A well regulated Militia, being necessary to the security of a free State, the right of the people to keep and bear Arms, shall not be infringed."

What does this mean to me as a citizen of the United States. Under this individual rights theory, this amendment restricts the legislative branch of the U. S. Government from passing any laws that prohibit the private possession of firearms. The reason this amendment was included in the Bill of Rights, which consist of the first ten amendments to the Constitution, was the possibility of an out-of-control government that tried to go against the will of the people. There are many who believe we are on the verge of an out-of-control government right now and this gives them an even more legitimate reason to hold on to these rights. They believe that the passage of any laws that restrict the rights to firearms ownership is a violation of the Constitution. I believe this is why most lawful gun owners in America are not really opposed to reasonable restrictions on gun ownership with the purpose of keeping them out of the hands those with mental issues or criminals.

It is the common practice of Governmental over-reach that scares the common man into believing that if they give the Government an inch that they will take a mile. They are not willing to give an inch on this issue because if they open the door to some restrictions then they have opened the door to allowing the Government to have complete control over all firearms. In America, the good ole boy is not going to go down without a fight. Based on this information I believe that a Christian should feel free to vote any way he chooses on this issue as long as they are informed of what the consequences are. I personally do not own a weapon, but I believe based on the scriptures that we have seen and the Second Amendment to the Constitution of the United States every person who is mentally sound and is not a convicted criminal should have that right. Therefore I would not vote for anyone who wants to enforce unreasonable gun laws. I will leave it to the individual to determine what is unreasonable. For some that would be any laws that restrict the ownership of any kind of firearm. For others it could be anything beyond the restriction of firearms only intended to be used by the military.

CHAPTER THIRTEEN
THE DRUG CRISIS

THE DRUG PROBLEM
THE COST OF ALCOHOL ADDICTION

In 2013, almost half of the 72,559 liver disease deaths, including those resulting specifically from cirrhosis of the liver, involved alcohol.

Excessive alcohol use results each year in approximately 2.5 million years of potential life lost or an average loss of thirty years for each fatality.

In 2010, more than 2.6 million hospitalizations were related to alcohol.

About one-third of deaths resulting from alcohol problems take the form of suicides and such accidents as head injuries, drowning incidents, and motor vehicle crashes.

About 20 percent of suicide victims in the United States involve people with alcohol problems.

In 2014, 30 percent of the country's fatal traffic incidents were related to alcohol-impaired driving.

Among youth, underage drinking is responsible for more than forty-three hundred deaths each year and one hundred eighty-nine thousand emergency room visits for alcohol-related injuries and other conditions.

Excessive drinking was responsible for one in ten deaths among adults between twenty and sixty-four years of age.

In 2010, the economic impact of excessive alcohol use in the United States approached an estimated $249 billion.

Alcoholism and Alcohol Abuse: Men vs. Women

Studies consistently demonstrate that more men than women struggle with alcoholism and alcohol abuse. While 5.7 million women are affected by an alcohol use disorder in the United States, nearly twice as many men—about 10.6 million—are affected. With a little less than 6 million women struggling with alcoholism, this gender discrepancy obviously shouldn't be taken to suggest that women are in the clear. Women may in fact need to be relatively more careful about their alcohol consumption because, due to gender differences in body structure and chemistry, which result in them effectively absorbing more alcohol from their drinks, women can become intoxicated more quickly than men when drinking comparable amounts of alcohol. In addition, women are more likely than men to experience problems related to alcohol, such as abusive relationships, unwanted sexual advances, and depression.

Health problems related to alcohol addiction and alcoholism vary, but they are of great concern because of their severity. For example, a Harvard School of Public Health study showed that having two or more drinks per day increases the risk of developing breast cancer. Heavy alcohol use directly affects brain function and has been shown to induce mental disorders such as mood, anxiety, psychotic, sleep, and dementia disorders.

In addition to mood and behavior changes, alcohol can affect thought, memory, and coordination. Excessive alcohol use can affect other organs such as the heart, liver, and pancreas, contributing to cardiomyopathy, irregular heartbeat, stroke, and high blood pressure.

Liver cirrhosis can occur from heavy drinking as can alcohol hepatitis and liver fibrosis.

Alcohol causes inflammation and swelling of the pancreas (pancreatitis), which can be painful and debilitating, and it can prevent proper digestion.

Alcohol abuse increases the risk of developing certain cancers of the mouth, esophagus, throat, liver, and breast as well as weakening the immune system, making the body more susceptible to various diseases like pneumonia and tuberculosis.

Aside from injury, violence, alcohol poisoning, susceptibility to certain diseases, and mental health problems, alcohol dependence or alcoholism can develop from long-term use and result in social problems, such as job loss, family issues, and lost productivity to name a few.

Pregnant women who drink are at risk for miscarriage, stillbirth, or fetal alcohol spectrum disorders.

Alcohol use can interact with certain medications, increasing the risk of additional health problems or even death.

In adolescents, alcohol use can interfere with brain development.

Excessive underage drinking has many consequences that affect college students across the United States, whether they choose to drink, including the following:

Consequences of Excessive Underage Drinking

Academic problems: Approximately 25 percent of college students reported falling behind, missing class, doing poorly on papers and exams, and receiving low grades as a result of drinking.

Alcohol abuse and dependence: About 20 percent of students meet the criteria for an alcohol use disorder.

Assault: About 696,000 students aged eighteen to twenty-four became victims of assault; the perpetrators in these cases were other students who had been drinking.

Death: About 1,825 college students aged eighteen to twenty-four die from unintentional injuries related to alcohol.

Drunk driving: About 85 percent of alcohol-impaired driving is associated with binge drinking.

Alcohol poisoning: Each year thousands of college students are transported to the emergency room because of alcohol poisoning, which can result in permanent brain damage or even death.

Health problems and suicide attempts: Suicide attempts are significantly higher in those who drink heavily compared with those who do not drink. Liver and other organ damage can result from long-term excessive drinking.

Injury: An estimated 10 percent of college students are injured because of drinking.

Police involvement: An estimated one hundred twelve thousand students were arrested for an alcohol-related offense in a single year.

Property damage and vandalism: Many colleges in the United States have major or moderate problems with property damage resulting from alcohol use; making these claims are more than 50 percent of administrators from colleges with high drinking levels among students and more than 25 percent of administrators from colleges with low student drinking levels.

Sexual abuse: Approximately ninety-seven thousand students aged eighteen to twenty-four reported experiencing sexual assault or date rape as a result of alcohol use.

Unsafe sex: An estimated 8 percent of college students had unprotected sex as a result of their drinking.

Given some of these consequences, it's clear that there is a strong relationship between crime and alcohol use. About three million violent crimes occur annually in the United States, and alcohol plays a role in 40 percent of them. Two-thirds of victims who have suffered domestic or partner violence reported there had been alcohol involved, and among cases of spousal violence, three out of four incidents involved an offender who had been under the influence of alcohol.

WHAT ARE THE EFFECTS OF DRUG ABUSE AND ADDICTION?

The consequences of drug abuse can be severe, destructive, and sometimes irreparable. Drug abuse and addiction can affect your life on every possible level, including socially, financially, occupationally, and health wise. A few reasons for this are that feeding a drug habit requires a lot of money, and being under the influence of drugs makes it difficult to honor your work obligations. The unrelenting cycle of high drug costs and incapacitation can lead to stealing, lying, or cheating to support your addiction.

Personal problems drug addiction sometimes lead to, may include the following:
1. Crime
2. Difficulty keeping a job and having other work-related problems
3. Homelessness
4. Contracting a disease(s)
5. Degeneration of physical and mental health
6. Conflicted relationships with loved ones
7. Isolation
8. Death

Certain drug abuse impacts your judgment and reaction time because these substances slow down your cognitive and motor functioning through various biological actions. Slow reaction time and impaired judgment can lead to a plethora of social and behavioral problems due to an inability to make rational decisions, including the following:

1. Physical violence
2. Risky sexual behaviors
3. Child abuse and neglect
4. Driving under the influence
5. Crime such as theft and prostitution
6. The spread of infectious diseases

One of the biggest problems drug addiction can cause is in your relationships with friends and family. Once you're in the grips of an unrelenting addiction, your personality changes because you believe the drug is an integral part of your survival. You make decisions while addicted that you would have never even entertained the thought of before your addiction.

If you have children, problems can include the following:
1. Forgetting to feed, wash, and dress your children
2. Exposing your children to harmful environments or people
3. Not paying rent, electric, water, and other essential bills
4. Abusing or neglecting your children's physical, emotional, and medical needs
5. Exposing your children to fights and conflict
6. Being unable to protect your children from accidents and other harm
7. Increasing the likelihood that your children will have a drug problem
8. Possibly having your children removed from your care by Child Protective Services

STATISTICS ON HEROINE ADDICTION AND ABUSE
An irreversible problem caused by opioid abuse is death by overdose, as evident in these statistics:
1. The number of heroin-overdose deaths has nearly tripled since 2010.
2. Heroin-overdose deaths were highest among adults between the ages of twenty-five and forty-four from 2000 to 2013.
3. In 2013, the rate of heroin overdose was four times higher in men than in women.
4. Between 2000 and 2013, the rate of overdose deaths involving heroin rose in each area across the country, with the Midwest experiencing the largest increase.

HOW DRUG ADDICTION AFFECTS YOUR HEALTH

Provided you avoid an accidental overdose, you will most likely experience other health-related issues as a result of your drug abuse. Certain drugs can cause specific types of health problems, given their chemical makeup and the way they are ingested or metabolized in the body. For example, methamphetamine can cause serious dental issues, while inhalants can destroy cells in the peripheral nervous system and brain.

Other diseases can result from the intravenous use of opioids, crack, and crystal meth, such as the following:
1. HIV
2. Hepatitis C (a liver virus that causes inflammation)
3. Cellulitis (a skin infection)
4. Endocarditis (an infection of the heart valves)

Drug addiction can also affect the health of those around you. Secondhand smoke has been well researched related to tobacco and is just the beginning in regard to illicit substances people commonly smoke. Presently, one study found that nonsmoking subjects exposed for an hour to high-THC marijuana in an unventilated space reported mild drug effects, and an additional study showed positive urine screens in subjects in the hours immediately after being exposed.

Also, engaging in unprotected sex after drug use exposes your partner to the infections listed above, and being under the influence of drugs makes it more likely that you will engage in risky sexual behaviors due to your impaired judgment.

If you're pregnant, drug use during pregnancy can cause your baby to be born with an addiction. This can lead to your baby experiencing severe withdrawal symptoms, known as neonatal abstinence syndrome (NAS), after he or she is born. Symptoms of NAS vary depending on what you used during pregnancy. Common symptoms can include seizures, restlessness, tremors, and difficulty eating and sleeping.

Along with physical health issues, your mental health can also be jeopardized by drug abuse. Many people who abuse substances also have a mental health disorder, such as depression or anxiety, and using drugs or alcohol can exacerbate the symptoms associated with these disorders. In some cases, substance abuse can be the cause of mental health issues.[6]

I included all of this article because of the extensive damage that is being done to our country. I believe there are a lot of reasons that these things are happening. Included in that list is the drug cartels and the legalization of drugs in the States. In the next chapter we will look at the possible solutions and discover why this is an important political topic.

---

[6] The previous statistics on alcohol and drug use in the US were provided by American Addiction Centers, Project Know.com. Written by Lauren Brande and edited by Meredith Watkins. Last updated October 19, 2021. 24/7 Hot line: (888) 830-7624

Chapter Fourteen
The Solution to the Drug Crisis

Alcohol Abuse Leads to Loss

Many years ago before I started my own business, I worked for a company that repaired aircraft components in a shop. When I was there, I knew a man who was very fond of his drink; and on numerous occasions, it seemed to cause problems for him and his family. He had a grown son I knew who had the same problem. Both of these men were my friends, and we spent a lot of time together.

One weekend the son decided he wanted to attend a gathering with me. There was plenty of social drinking going on, but the young man, just like his father, had trouble knowing when he needed to stop. When I began to see there was going to be a problem, I asked him for the keys to his car, and he gave them to me. Later in the evening, he became out of control. He made a very snide remark to one of the ladies there that irritated her husband. Her husband was a great guy, but he was big, strong, and not someone you wanted angry at you.

The young man was too drunk to know what he was doing, but it was obvious to everyone else there. He continued to stir up trouble, and the big guy was really getting angry. I told the young man he needed to stop talking before he got himself in a jam, but he got mad and demanded his keys. This put me in a precarious situation because this was my friend's son, but I refused to give him the keys, and he became furious. He came at me, declaring that he would take his keys away from me no matter what it took, so I slapped him across the face. He sat back down in his chair and remained quiet until he fell asleep.

I had solved the current crisis, but I was concerned about what would happen when he told his dad what I had done. I waited for the shoe to drop the whole following week, but life went on as normal like nothing had ever happened. After about a week, I found an opportunity when I was alone with the father. I asked him whether his son had said anything to him about what had happened over that weekend. He said no; he hadn't said anything. Then he asked me what had happened. I told him the whole story and waited for a bad reaction. This is what he said: "It's about time somebody put that boy in his place." None of us ever mentioned the event again.

I could tell many other stories like this as I'm sure most of you can as well. Alcohol and drug abuse are very large issues in America, and the problem is getting bigger every day. This shouldn't be the case among Christians. I'm not criticizing these individuals who have fallen into this snare of the devil. They are victims. But this is such an easy trap to fall into, and many people are genetically more susceptible to the addiction than others. If you are one of those people who are susceptible to this snare, then you should take proper precautions to avoid it. Alcohol is a grave problem in America, but drugs is becoming a bigger problem. The Bible doesn't really say much about drugs because back then they didn't exist like they do now. I believe it is appropriate, as far as the Bible is concerned to place all substance abuse in the same category.

DEGRADATION

I believe the use and abuse of drugs and alcohol basically fall into 4 categories according to my Biblical research.

1. Alcohol provided the occasion to allow sin.

The misuse of alcohol has very early beginnings in the Bible and has resulted in the degradation of moral character and personal standards or prohibitions since the beginning. In this first example, we will look at Noah, whom we all know as a great man of God. He was used in an amazing way to save all mankind when God destroyed all life with the flood. Yet through the use of alcohol, Noah became an instrument of sin. After God blessed him following the flood, He used the blessings as an occasion to celebrate by drinking wine. In the verses below we will see that drinking to celebrate God's blessings to the point of having a glad heart is not a sin. Noah went too far with the wine, however, and got drunk and passed out.

Because of this drunkenness, he was unaware of his surroundings and was passed out drunk on his bed. This situation allowed his son Ham to see his nakedness, which resulted in the curse on Canaan. (In the Bible, the words "to uncover one's nakedness" normally means there was a sexual sin committed.) In this situation, alcohol didn't directly cause the sin, which Ham committed, but it did cause the conditions leading to the sin. The alcohol made Noah vulnerable.

I believe this is an illustration to us that if we go to a celebration, even with no ill intent, and allow ourselves to go too far with strong drink, we may open an opportunity for sin to be the end result. When a husband or wife starts out with a small drink to celebrate or relax, it may be all innocent at first. But if they aren't able to stop with just a drink or two, it often ends up turning into spousal abuse or worse. Ladies, when you go out and celebrate with your friends and allow yourselves to go too far with alcohol, you put yourselves in a position of vulnerability. The definition of *vulnerable* is susceptible to physical or emotional attack or harm.

> And the sons of Noah, that went forth of the ark, were Shem, and Ham, and Japheth: and Ham is the father of Canaan. These are the three sons of Noah: and of them was the whole earth overspread. And Noah began to be an husbandman, and he planted a vineyard: And he drank of the wine, and was drunken; and he was uncovered within his tent. And Ham, the father of Canaan, saw the nakedness of his father, and told his two brethren without. And Shem and Japheth took a garment, and laid it upon both their shoulders, and went backward, and covered the nakedness of their father; and their faces were backward, and they saw not their father's nakedness. And Noah awoke from his wine, and knew what his younger son had done unto him. And he said, Cursed be

Canaan; a servant of servants shall he be unto his brethren. And he said, Blessed be the LORD God of Shem; and Canaan shall be his servant. (Gen. 9:18–26)

2. Alcohol was used to intentionally deceive Lot, resulting in sin.

The second example involves the daughters of Lot, Abraham's brother's son, who was also a God-fearing man and was saved from the destruction of Sodom and Gomorrah along with his two daughters. He was also deceived by alcohol. In this example, however, alcohol was used specifically for this purpose. The daughters of Lot, believing their father's bloodline would end with his passing, devised a plan to get their father drunk and take advantage of him to get pregnant. Being a man of God, Lot would never have gone along with this plan, but apparently the daughters didn't care about that. This was the use of alcohol with the intent of taking advantage of someone. This is the same as using what they call a date rape drug or intentionally getting someone drunk with the intentions of taking advantage of them.

I believe in both of these cases that the persons who became drunk were the victims. One caused himself to become vulnerable by abusing the alcohol on his own, and the other became vulnerable by putting himself in a position where someone else could take advantage of him. I'm not suggesting in any way that when someone gets taken advantage of that he or she brought it upon themselves. I'm just pointing out the fact that we should be aware of our surroundings and be careful of what situations we allow ourselves to be put in and what kind of people we hang out with. But most of all, we should be aware of how much alcohol or other drugs we allow to influence us.

If you have enough alcohol in your system that it makes you unaware of your surroundings, makes you lower your moral standards, or causes you to allow people to influence you to do what you normally wouldn't do, then you have exceeded what is considered acceptable to God. If so, then you went too far. As for drugs, they are used in the same way. The main difference between drugs and alcohol is the fact that several drinks are needed to get in this condition, but it may take only a very small amount of drugs to have the same effect. Incidentally, this verse also proves that it's possible for a man to be raped. Many people think it's impossible for a man to be raped, but that isn't true.

This is just a side note, but I mentioned that this happened after Sodom and Gomorrah were destroyed due to their immorality. Could it be that Lot's daughters had been influenced toward evil thinking because of the place where they grew up and the people they had been exposed to? It's also interesting to note that Ham, Noah's son, took advantage of him right after God destroyed every living thing off the face of the earth because of sin and corruption. Incidental? I don't think so! Just saying.

> And Lot went up out of Zoar, and dwelt in the mountain, and his two daughters with

him; for he feared to dwell in Zoar: and he dwelt in a cave, he and his two daughters. And the firstborn said unto the younger, Our father is old, and there is not a man in the earth to come in unto us after the manner of all the earth: Come, let us make our father drink wine, and we will lie with him, that we may preserve seed of our father. And they made their father drink wine that night: and the firstborn went in, and lay with her father; and he perceived not when she lay down, nor when she arose. And it came to pass on the morrow, that the firstborn said unto the younger, Behold, I lay yesternight with my father: let us make him drink wine this night also; and go thou in, and lie with him, that we may preserve seed of our father. And they made their father drink wine that night also: and the younger arose, and lay with him; and he perceived not when she lay down, nor when she arose. Thus were both the daughters of Lot with child by their father. And the first born bare a son, and called his name Moab: the same is the father of the Moabites unto this day. And the younger, she also bare a son, and called his name Benammi: the same is the father of the children of Ammon unto this day. (Gen. 19:30–38)

3. Alcohol was used to steal what rightfully belonged to someone else.

In Genesis 27:23–29, Jacob used alcohol to deceive his father Isaac, so he could steal his brother's blessing. In Proverbs 4:14–17, alcohol is associated with evil and violence. In Proverbs 20:1, alcohol is described as a deceiver (mocker) and being unwise. In Isaiah 28:7, it is associated with poor judgment. In Isaiah 5:11–17, it is associated with destruction.

> Who hath woe? who hath sorrow? who hath contentions? who hath babbling? who hath wounds without cause? who hath redness of eyes? They that tarry long at the wine; they that go to seek mixed wine. Look not thou upon the wine when it is red, when it giveth his colour in the cup, when it moveth itself aright. At the last it biteth like a serpent, and stingeth like an adder. Thine eyes shall behold strange women, and thine heart shall utter perverse things. Yea, thou shalt be as he that lieth down in the midst of the sea, or as he that lieth upon the top of a mast. They have stricken me, shalt thou say, and I was not sick; they have beaten me, and I felt it not: when shall I awake? I will seek it yet again. (Prov. 23:29–35)

Have you ever seen a better description of an alcoholic? The addiction is even worse with drugs. Who ends up sorrowful? Who starts conflicts? Who says things that don't make sense? Who gets hurt all the time for no reason? Who gets lured by the harlot?

Who utters vulgarity? Who placed himself or herself in harm's way? Who feels sick when there is nothing wrong with him or her? Who takes a beating and feels no pain? Who after all that, when he or she wakes up, even knowing what is going to happen, seeks it yet again?

4. Alcohol was used to medically treat someone (medication).

In the following verses, alcohol could be considered a use of medication due to the dire circumstances described. I don't believe this qualifies as a major category, however, because, especially today, there are other resources available to assist people in these areas. What most people fail to recognize is the fact that alcohol is a depressant. It may make you have a merry heart for a short time, but the result leaves you worse off than when you started.

> It is not for kings, O Lemuel, it is not for kings to drink wine; nor for princes strong drink: Lest they drink, and forget the law, and pervert the judgment of any of the afflicted. Give strong drink unto him that is ready to perish, and wine unto those that be of heavy hearts. Let him drink, and forget his poverty, and remember his misery no more (Prov. 31:4–7).

I used to object to the use of drugs in any sort of way, but in light of what the scripture says here, perhaps it does have its proper use. According to these verses, the legal use of drugs to treat people for depression could be considered legitimate. I think this would need to be clinically diagnosed depression and the drugs would need to be prescribed by a doctor with specific terms of use. It is a fact that the recreational use of marijuana usually leads to other more addictive drug use. This verse describes these people as being ready to perish. (This is someone who is depressed to the point of being suicidal or perhaps terminally ill and ready to die.) It also says for those who are of a heavy heart. (This could be someone who suffered a major loss in his or her life and desperately needed some relief from mental anguish.) This can be caused by the death of a loved one or maybe even a great loss during a divorce. Finally, it refers to those who suffer from excessive poverty or misery. This could be someone who is starving to death, and there is no one to help him or her survive or someone who is in misery for some other reason.

Alcohol and or other drugs can help people in certain situations, but these situations should be considered necessary medical treatments, with alcohol or drugs being properly distributed and monitored. Alcohol and drugs, like most other things in life, can be used for good. Unfortunately, they can also be abused, and that is when they cause sinful behaviour. In any case, though anyone can fall victim to these adverse situations, hopefully this doesn't describe the physical or mental condition of most Christians. I think it's interesting that the verse says those who are "ready to perish." To perish means to suffer everlasting death or cease to exist in the presence of

God. Christians, according to God's Word, don't perish. They are asleep in Christ until the resurrection.

STOP LAWLESSNESS

I don't believe there is any question about whether we have a drug and alcohol abuse problem in America. The problem we cannot get anyone to agree on is how we should deal with this problem. It is interesting to me that this seems to be divided along political Party lines just like every other issue that we have discussed. One Party seems to believe that the best way to deal with crime is to call it something other than crime. I guess that is one way to make friends with the criminals (win their votes), solve the prison crowding problem (win their votes) bring down the crime rate statistics (win the countries votes) and tell everyone that it isn't their fault that they are addicted to drugs (win the public's vote). Here is what I think; I don't believe we should be trying to make friends with the criminals. Criminals do not care about who they hurt and if they are not punished for their crimes they will not stop committing them. The laws that have been passed to legalize drugs in many States may make the books look good statistically speaking, but the actual crime rate has risen substantially. If we make marijuana legal then we can empty the prisons and make the crime rate go down true, but what are we doing to the law-abiding citizens in the mean time. Where drug use goes up the actual crime rate goes up and that includes the use of marijuana. It isn't that hard to figure out that drug use lowers inhibitions and moral standards therefore freeing the conscience of any sense of wrong doing. To the drug addict stealing is not wrong, vandalism is not wrong, starting fights over nothing is not wrong and even shooting someone is not wrong any longer to this person because their conscience has been nullified. They are often not aware of what they are doing much less being concerned about whether it is wrong or not.

Many States have passed laws saying that if you don't have more than a certain amount of drugs on you when you get caught then it is legal. So let me ask you; is a little bit of cyanide alright? Is a little bit of stealing alright? Is a little bit of cheating by your spouse alright? Is a little bit of murder alright? Where do we draw the limit? Legalizing drugs may bring down the statistical crime rate and it may help resolve the issue of prison overcrowding, but what is doing to the people of your community. All of this is just simply legalizing lawlessness. Using drugs is breaking the law the same as any other crime. The laws are written in order to protect people from themselves and from other people. Every time you let a criminal go you are putting that person and everyone else round that person in danger. You say that a small amount of drugs doesn't hurt anyone and so we should leave that person alone and only go after the dealers. Okay, if a little bit of drugs and a little bit of personal drug use shouldn't be considered breaking the law because it doesn't hurt anyone then why are we going after the dealers? If the drugs don't hurt anyone then what is wrong with buying and selling them? The truth is even a little bit of drug use is a problem. You just saw the statistics from the American Addiction Centers. Do you think all of these social problems are only caused by people with large amounts of drugs on them? It only takes a small amount of drugs over an extended period of time to become addicted. It only takes a small amount of drugs to cause an overdose. It only takes a small amount of drugs to create all of these statistics. The truth is that these States are only legalizing drugs for two reasons. First, these States are only legalizing drug use under strict State guidelines and controls. What does that mean? The States have figured out that if they legalize drugs then they can be rich like the drug dealers are. Legalizing drugs means big dollars for the State. Second, they are legalizing drugs to win popularity with the criminals. Why? This is because criminals can help politicians to win elections just like anyone else. A certain political Party recently verified this by proposing the legalization of incarcerated criminals to vote again.

THE RESULTS OF LAWLESSNESS

Ask the business owners in city of Portland Oregon how well this legalization of lawlessness is working out for them? The city leaders are still not going to admit that they made any mistakes going down this destructive path, but the business owners and the law abiding citizens in the city will tell you. Illegal drug use is happening on every street corner every day. The crime rate is going through the roof. Homelessness, despite significant efforts by the city leaders is completely out of control. Drug overdoses occur daily. Murder is rising rapidly. The amount of stealing and vandalism has risen to the point that many national store chains are closing their stores and moving out of the city. The insurance rates on homes and vehicles are sky rocketing out of control. The answer is to crack down on crime and stop legalizing lawlessness. I could give you plenty of scriptures from God's Word that that show that the Government is responsible for maintaining order in our society, but if you are a Christian you already know this. The only way to get our cities back on track and to get a handle on the drug abuse problem in our country is to crack down on crime and keep criminals in jail or prison where they belong. I'm not against programs that are designed to help people with drug problems, but you must first convince the person that what they are doing is wrong and that they need help. You cannot help someone with a drug problem if they don't want to be helped. How should a Christian vote on these issues; by voting for those politicians that will pass laws that will stop lawlessness, stop drug use, stop legalizing drugs. If we can convince people on drugs that they need help by keeping them in jail or prison, then we have helped the person addicted to the drugs as well as cleaned up the community. So, yes it may not make us popular with the criminals, it may not help the crime rate statistics look good, but it will help with drug addiction and homelessness and lawlessness. If you are looking for a way to change these things, then vote for someone who will stop the States from passing laws that are contradictory to Federal laws. I can understand the State making the disciplinary portion of a law more severe or even making a law more restrictive, but how can a State legalize something that is a Federal crime?

One other thing I'd like to mention on this topic concerning the intent of the law. The number one objection of the re-criminalization of drug possession and use is the groups that suggest that this re-criminalization would result in the discrimination of minorities. I don't think laws should be based on racial profiling. Let me give you an example of what they mean. In the prisons today the ratio of individuals incarcerated by race is as follows: Black or African American 39%, Hispanic or Latino 37% and Whites 22%. The percentage of the population by race is Black 12.5%, Hispanic 18.5% and White 60.1%. Because of this they say that more blacks will be punished for this crime than whites. These percentages are based on the last census taking in the U.S. That means that based on how many Blacks there are in the U.S a higher percentage of them will be incarcerated for drugs related offenses than whites. But let's look at the actual numbers by using these percentages in relation to the number of people in the U.S. 60.1% of 334,233,854 (U.S. population in 2023) = 200,540,312 x 22% = 44,118,869 Whites in prison, 334,233,854 x 12.5% = 41,779,232 x 39% = 16,293,900 Blacks in prison, 334,233,854 x 18.5% = 61,833,263 x 37% = 22,878,307 Hispanics in prison. According to my calculations that means there are actually 21,240,562 more Whites in prison for drug related charges than Hispanics and 27,824,969 more Whites than Blacks. The percentage of a certain race that is prosecuted for a crime should not be a determining factor as to whether this is a crime or not. If laws become based on racial percentages then the laws are discriminatory. Laws should not be based on race, religion or gender any more than they are based on popularity. The laws are created to protect people from themselves and others and these other factors should not influence the validity of the law. We should not get in the habit of legalizing lawlessness (harmful behavior) for any reason. Baretta (Robert Blake) used to say on the TV show "Don't do the crime if you can't do the time".

CHAPTER FIFTEEN
STUDENT DEBT FORGIVENESS

STUDENT DEBT FORGIVENESS IS ALL ABOUT KEEPING POWER

This is a political stunt that the Democratic Party Conjured up in order to win the college student vote during the 2020 election. Everyone knows that the college vote is a large group to get on-board. The problem has always been trying to figure out a way to do that. Historically speaking the young adult college age citizen is one of the most difficult to get involved in the Democratic process. Most of them feel either they do not have any interest in politics or, even if they voted it wouldn't make any difference. Most college students simply do not have any interest in politics and they can't even tell you who President Trump is or who the current vice president is. This is sad, but it also opens the door to millions of votes that are up for grabs to the candidate that has the best way to solicit their votes. These college students, if they could be convince to vote for a particular candidate, could easily change the results of a general election. The candy that was dangled in front of them was a way to have their college paid for by the Government. This is simply buying votes. I know that the economy is tough and it is hard to go to college and pay the bills. I know because I did it myself with a wife and five sons. What better way could there possibly be to entice young adults into voting for you other than letting them get out of paying for a debt that they owe. In the last couple elections college students have been voting at record levels. In the 2020 election 66% of the college students who were registered to vote actually did cast a ballot. This is an increase of 14% over the 2016 election. During the 2018 midterm election college student vote doubled from 19% in 2014 to 40%. Some say that this increase was partially due to the President Donald Trump era, but most believe it had more to do with the recent get-out-to-vote initiatives conducted in colleges across the country. I am not suggesting that more college students voting is a bad thing. I believe every American citizen should be involved in the Democratic process by casting their ballots. What concerns me is the fact that these votes are being bought by political brides that our country can't afford. Biden made these promises to forgive student debt and start a trend headed towards the Government paying for all college cost without even knowing whether or not he could legally keep them. These college students are easy targets for false promises since they are new to the Democratic process and therefore more susceptible to political stunts. I am not saying that college students are not intelligent enough to make good political choices. What I am saying is that most college students are pre-occupied with their educational goals and do not have the time needed to research and understand the majority of the political issues at hand. This opens them up to being talked into voting blindly by trusting someone else who has talked them into voting a certain way. The forgiveness of all my debt would certainly be a persuasive incentive on the surface. [7]

---

[7] Analysis by Maricruz Ariana Osorio and Melissa R. Michelson August 30, 2022 at 7:00 am EDT

LIBERAL EDUCATORS

In our colleges today the students are being educated by those who believe they are too intelligent to believe in a creator. Since they are being taught by the professors to be atheist, then why should they be concerned about being a responsible adult and paying the bills that they have accumulated? These college students are essentially being trained to be irresponsible in my opinion. If there is no God and our country is promoting lawlessness, then why should we be concerned about repaying our debt? Even the Government doesn't pay its debt why should we? With the country already being 33 trillion dollars in debt and no intentions on paying it back why shouldn't we get in on the action? If you have no moral compass and no conviction, and no concern about what God or the Bible says about being responsible, then you are absolutely right in your thinking.

FREE EDUCATION FOR ALL

Student debt forgiveness is where it starts. Where it is headed is free college for everyone. The truth is it isn't fair to pay for college for some and not for all. To be frank, what about those who have already been through college and had to pay for it themselves; shouldn't the Government be responsible to give them a considerable refund check? If the government is going to be responsible for those who are in college now then doesn't that require them to be responsible for paying for the education of everyone else in the future? In May each year is the National College

Decision Day. That is the day that 2 million college students and their parents decide what college they will go to and how they will pay for it. Historically the overwhelming majority, two thirds of college student parents in the past, have felt like it was their responsibility to pay for their child's education including college. Up until round 2010 Americans believed deeply in self-reliance and individual responsibility. Slowly this trend is changing along with every other sign of independence and responsible behaviour that we used to expect from all Americans. This way of thinking had not changed much since the first survey on the topic back in the 1980s. By 2015 that opinion had changed dramatically and approximately 50% of those parents at that time believed that the Government should at least help out with these educational related expenses. That is virtually the same results that were found again in 2019 and 2020. Americas more than ever now believe that the Government should have substantial responsibility for funding higher education.[8]

TEACHING MORALITY AND RESPONSIBILITY

President Biden has taken advantage of this fact and offered college students something that he doesn't have the authority to produce. Now the majority of those who thought they had been granted this debt forgiveness and proceeded to redirect those funds, are finding themselves in a financial pinch trying to

---

[8] Analysis by Natasha Quadlin and Brian Powell April 25, 2022 at 7:00 am EDT

correct the situation and get back on track. President Biden, only after being cut down by the Supreme Court, has admitted to his error and is now scrambling to find ways to help these college students get relief from the pinch he put them in. The thing we need to learn from this is the people in our country must come back to God and must come back to being responsible adults that make decisions based on morality and godly principals. We should not be promising get out of jail free cards and get rich quick schemes and get out of paying your debt free alternatives. Our children need to be taught to be responsible for the debt that they accumulate and so should our country. President Biden is still trying to find loop holes in the law to continue to provide bail outs for college students. He has still managed to erase $127 billion in student debt so far for more than 3.5 million borrowers. He is using existing programs that were previously hard to access to deliver this relief.[9]

In the mean time what is happening to the national debt? If you are a Christian you should be voting for a candidate that is concerned about the out of control spending and the false promises made in an effort to buy votes. We would all like for the college student debt to be forgiven and for all future education to be free and for all medical expenses to be covered for free, but that is ignoring reality and promoting irresponsibility.

---

[9] www.cnbc.com, 2023/10/29

Chapter Sixteen
Climate Change

The Far Right on Climate Change

The ultra conservative will come right out and tell you that what they use to call Global warming is just a hoax. The reason they changed from calling it global warming to climate change is because anyone with any common sense can see that we are breaking records now that were set way back in the 30s and 40s. If the globe is warming the world at the rate that these people are claiming, then those records should have broken a long time ago. Breaking records from the 20s, 30s and 40s doesn't scream global warming to me. Instead it is telling me that around sixty or seventy years ago we had temperatures that were hotter than it is now. If the global warming is causing the world to get hotter every year, then why are we proving every year that once before it was even hotter than it is now? Not only that, but every year we also break cold temperature records that were set 70 years ago. If the Globe is warming every year how can we be setting colder than ever recorded temperatures as well? I don't need to be scientist to see and understand that what they are telling us about the weather isn't true. Tell me whose pollution was responsible for the drought in the days of Joseph in Egypt when all the people on the earth had to go to Egypt to buy food because of the seven year drought that the Pharaoh had dreamed about?

Take a look at the statistics over the last few decades on the number of people that have died as a result of natural disasters. The following statistics are a result of the research from Hanah Ritchie, Pablo Rasado and Max Roser in 2022, see reference below. On average natural disasters are responsible for approximately 45000 deaths per year. Deaths from natural disasters have seen a large decline over the last century. It has declined from millions of deaths per year in the early 1900s to around 60,000 in the last decade. In the late 1920s there were 3.0 to 3.5 million deaths caused by natural disasters such as geophysical, meteorological, and climate events including earth quakes, volcanic activity, landslides, drought, wildfires, and storms and flooding. Since 1960 there has not been one decade where more than 500,000 were killed by natural disasters. In the early 1900s the annual average number of deaths was in the 400,000 to 500,000 range. In the second half of the century and into the 2000s the death toll annually has been less than 100,000. [10]

I believe this is why they are no longer saying Global warming and are now calling it climate change. I'm not going to go as far as to say that fossil fuels aren't causing any damage to the earth, I'm sure they are. But so are garbage dumps and septic tanks and even cows so they say. If the world is so concerned about climate change, then why is it that the Unites States seems to be the only nation trying to do anything about it? China is by far the largest producer of greenhouse gases accounting for more that 10,065

---

[10] Hanah Ritchie, Pablo Rosado and Max Roser (2022) – "Natural Disasters", Published online at OurWorldInData.org. Retreived from:'https://ourworldindata.org/natural-disasters' (Online Resource)

million tons of CO2 released into the atmosphere. This is almost double that of any other country, and yet they have only in the last few years made any effort to change their policies. The United States withdrew from the Paris climate accord because of the terms of the agreement that caused unfair economic burden imposed on American workers and businesses by U.S. pledges made under the agreement. These same pledges were not enforced by any other countries.

THE EARTH WAS CREATED FOR MAN

Adam and Eve were placed in the Garden of Eden for their benefit, not for the benefit of the garden. They were expected to tend to the garden just as we are expected to take care of our environment, but it is clear that the environment was created for them not the other way around. Mankind is without question God's greatest creation and God placed them in the Garden of Eden so they could live the good life. The question isn't whether or not man should take care of the earth that we live on, I think we all believe that. The point is that the earth and the trees and the plants and the animals were created to support the life of the man.

> And God said, Let the waters bring forth abundantly the moving creature that hath life, and fowl that may fly above the earth in the open firmament of heaven. And God created great whales, and every living creature that moveth, which the waters brought forth abundantly, after their kind, and every winged fowl after his kind: and

God saw that it was good. And God blessed them, saying, Be fruitful, and multiply, and fill the waters in the seas, and let fowl multiply in the earth. And the evening and the morning were the fifth day. And God said, Let the earth bring forth the living creature after his kind, cattle, and creeping thing, and beast of the earth after his kind: and it was so. And God made the beast of the earth after his kind, and cattle after their kind, and every thing that creepeth upon the earth after his kind: and God saw that it was good. And God said, Let us make man in our image, after our likeness: and let them have dominion over the fish of the sea, and over the fowl of the air, and over the cattle, and over all the earth, and over every creeping thing that creepeth upon the earth. So God created man in his own image, in the image of God created he him; male and female created he them. And God blessed them, and God said unto them, Be fruitful, and multiply, and replenish the earth, and subdue it: and have dominion over the fish of the sea, and over the fowl of the air, and over every living thing that moveth upon the earth. And God said, Behold, I have given you every herb bearing seed, which is upon the face of all the earth, and every tree, in the which is the fruit of a tree yielding seed; to you it shall be for meat. And to every beast of the earth, and to every fowl of the air, and to every thing that creepeth upon the earth, wherein there is life, I have given every green herb for meat: and it was so. (Gen 1:20-30)

Before the fall of man the ground did not even have to be worked to produce its fruits. The fact is the earth was created to support man and when it was created it was capable of doing that without any help from man at all. Because of the fall of man the Bible says that the earth or the ground was cursed so that man would have to work the ground and by the sweat of thy face thou shalt eat bread to make the ground produce as it did before then. It is true that the earth is cursed because of the sin of man, but that happened in the very beginning not by the hands of coal workers, the loggers and oil rigs. All of those things were created by God in order to be used by man to support their needs. I have no doubt that we could find cleaner and less harmful ways to produce some of these things, but we need to figure out how to do it without harming families.

> And he said, Who told thee that thou wast naked? Hast thou eaten of the tree, whereof I commanded thee that thou shouldest not eat? And the man said, The woman whom thou gavest to be with me, she gave me of the tree, and I did eat. And the LORD God said unto the woman, What is this that thou hast done? And the woman said, The serpent beguiled me, and I did eat. And the LORD God said unto the serpent,

Because thou hast done this, thou art cursed above all cattle, and above every beast of the field; upon thy belly shalt thou go, and dust shalt thou eat all the days of thy life: And I will put enmity between thee and the woman, and between thy seed and her seed; it shall bruise thy head, and thou shalt bruise his heel. Unto the woman he said, I will greatly multiply thy sorrow and thy conception; in sorrow thou shalt bring forth children; and thy desire shall be to thy husband, and he shall rule over thee. And unto Adam he said, Because thou hast hearkened unto the voice of thy wife, and hast eaten of the tree, of which I commanded thee, saying, Thou shalt not eat of it: cursed is the ground for thy sake; in sorrow shalt thou eat of it all the days of thy life; Thorns also and thistles shall it bring forth to thee; and thou shalt eat the herb of the field; In the sweat of thy face shalt thou eat bread, till thou return unto the ground; for out of it wast thou taken: for dust thou art, and unto dust shalt thou return. And Adam called his wife's name Eve; because she was the mother of all living. Unto Adam also and to his wife did the LORD God make coats of skins, and clothed them. And the LORD God said, Behold, the man is become as one of us, to know good and evil: and now, lest he put forth his hand, and take also of the tree of life, and eat, and live for ever:

> Therefore the LORD God sent him forth from the garden of Eden, to till the ground from whence he was taken. So he drove out the man; and he placed at the east of the garden of Eden Cherubims, and a flaming sword which turned every way, to keep the way of the tree of life. (Gen 3:11-24)

The whole issue is not based on the question as to whether we should not destroy the environment with human waste and abuses. The issue is that the tree huggers want to place more emphases on plants and animals than on human life. The fact is the earth was created to support the man not man the earth and the plants and animals were put here to feed the man not for the man to support the plants and animals. We do not believe that people should be losing their livelihood to preserve a bird's habitat or that thousands of coal miners should lose their jobs so a politician can win the vote of the tree hugger. I am not suggesting that man should not take care of the planet; after all it is our home. I'm only saying that the home was built for the family, not the family for the home. It sort of reminds me of the verse where Jesus told the Pharisees that the Sabbath was made for man, not man for the Sabbath.(Mk 2:27-28) Never-the-less, I know that God expects us to take care of our homes, but I believe this can be accomplished without punishing mankind.

TAKING CARE OF OUR HOME

> And the LORD God planted a garden eastward in Eden; and there he put the man whom he had formed. (Gen 2:8)

> And the LORD God took the man, and put him into the garden of Eden to dress it and to keep it. (Gen 2:15)

When I was growing up I probably spent more time outside and in the woods than most people. I grew up hunting and camping and doing all those outside activities. My Dad and my brothers and I went camping almost every weekend. We were always taught that we should, not just leave every place that we went to like it was when we got there, but that we should leave it better than it was when we got there. It still bothers me to see people throw trash out their window going down the road, even if they say it is biodegradable. That means that eventually the mess will go away on its own naturally, but that doesn't change the fact that it looks dirty until it does which can take a long time. I remember once stopping at a convenience store to pick up something and when I went back out and got in my vehicle I saw the people in the car next to me dumping their ashtrays out on the ground in the parking lot. It discussed me so bad that I got back out of my car and went back in the store and told the people in the store what they were doing. The people in the store just looked at me like there was something wrong with me and said, "uh, Okay". So I went back out and picked up all the butts off the ground and threw them in the trash myself. Trust me, I believe in taking care of the environment, but I don't believe the needs of the environment should outweigh the needs of the people that God created the environment to support in the first place.

I believe the Christian or evangelical vote should be cast in favor of those who are concerned about the environment, but they do not harm families in the effort to solve the problem. The earth is not more important than the people it was created to support. Let us find ways to clean up the environment without hurting people. I don't think whether a politician believes in climate change or not, is as important as whether they believe in putting the welfare of people ahead of the welfare of the planet, but both should be taken into consideration. I know that the hardcore right will say that anyone who believes in climate change is not an option. This is because of the stands that these politicians have taken in the past that have harmed families. I understand that, but I don't think philosophy is as important as policy. With that being said, most presidents have historically supported the philosophy of their political party once they were in office and even if they didn't, the president doesn't makes these decisions by himself.

Chapter Seventeen
The Economy

Are you better off Today

Who reading this book today can honestly say they are better off economically speaking, now under President Biden, than they were under president Trump just a few years ago? I know that there are a lot of reasons why the average American is suffering today and I can't even say that it is President Biden's fault. I have a sign in my office that says, "I never said it was your fault, I said I was going to blame you". I believe this is the attitude of the average American voter. If you don't believe this is true, then just look at President Biden's recent poles. Even though he talks a lot about how much he has done for the economy, people are hurting and they just aren't buying his rhetoric. Don't tell me all you have done to make my life less stressful, make my life less stressful.

The Liberal Philosophy

Most people who care anything about politics know and understand the basic difference in philosophy between the liberal and the conservative. I always think of the quote from Winston Churchill, or Edmund Burke, since both are accredited for the phrase, that says:

> "If you are not a liberal at 25, you have no heart. If you are not a conservative at 35 you have no brain."

This quote lays down the groundwork for the liberal and conservative argument in my opinion. Liberals believe in over taxing the wealthy (Successful) to give to those who have not succeeded regardless of the reason. Conservatives believe in Capitalism which is often referred to as "The Trickle Down Theory". That is they believe that if they can create an environment that makes it easier for people to be successful then this will create more jobs and more opportunities for those who otherwise wouldn't have them. The liberal mind, as good intentions would dictate, believes that everyone should be given the same opportunity to succeed and not based on their own ability or effort, but if they can't or won't become successful through their own efforts, then they should be supported by the success of others. Another word for this is Democratic Socialism. We discussed this previously and I can see why this philosophy is popular with the young people especially. This type of economy would guarantee their success in life whether they were personally willing to put forth the effort to be successful or not. This explains the attitude of being a dedicated liberal, or socialist, at 25 since in entails the success of every person regardless of their personal ability or effort and these young people have thus far invested very little in their own success. They believe that the Government should take care of their every need such as medical care, education, employment and anything else they think they need or want.

The problem with this way of thinking is all of those things cost billions of dollars that the government doesn't have. So how do they get the money to do these things? The only way is take it away from those individuals and companies that have made the effort and the sacrifices to be successful. This is done by taxing, in other words, penalizing those who have done the work to reward those who have not. Granted the Bible teaches us that we should not only be willing to help the poor and the disadvantaged and the mentally ill, but we should give with joy. The key is we should give willingly, not have it taken away from us. If we give willingly then we can ensure that the funds that we have given are going where we want them to. When the Government takes it then we have no say so about where the funds go. I am willing to help those who can't help themselves and I often do. I am not willing to give to those who could provide for themselves, but they don't. I would try to help those who lost their jobs and are actively trying to find another one and are doing any kind of work they can find in the mean time, but I am not willing to help those who claim that they can't find a job when they are not trying to find work and all they do is sit at home all day and draw unemployment for as long as they can get away with it.

What kind of lesson are we teaching them when the Government will pay them to stay home more than they made when they were working. What are we teaching them when we do not require them to be actively seeking employment while they are collecting unemployment? The Government should at least be requiring these people to be working or be in training for some kind of work. What kind of Government tells them we will help you if you stay unemployed altogether, but if you start making any money at all we are not going to help you anymore. You wonder why people stay home instead of going out and trying to find any job that will help. If they don't find a job that can support the standard of living that they are accustomed to then they won't take any job because the Government will pay them more than they can make to stay home and will take away any help if they work at all. The truth is the Government wants everyone to be supported by them. They want everyone to work for the Government regardless of what their job is. The reason is because this is how Democratic socialism works. If we get everyone to work for the Government, and everyone to be supported by the Government, then we have created a socialistic society. This gives the Government complete control over the people. What happened to a Government of the people, by the people and for the people? The people of this country have turned control of this country over to the liberals. What does the Bible say about this?

> For yourselves know how ye ought to follow us: for we behaved not ourselves disorderly among you; Neither did we eat any man's bread for nought; but wrought with labour and travail night and day, that we might not be chargeable to any of you: Not because we have not power, but to make ourselves an ensample unto you to follow us. For even when we were with you, this we commanded you, that if any would not

work, neither should he eat. For we hear that there are some which walk among you disorderly, working not at all, but are busybodies. Now them that are such we command and exhort by our Lord Jesus Christ, that with quietness they work, and eat their own bread. But ye, brethren, be not weary in well doing. And if any man obey not our word by this epistle, note that man, and have no company with him, that he may be ashamed. (2Thess 3:7-14)

THE CONSERVATIVE PHILOSOPHY

Now what about the conservative philosophy? Churchill said, "If you are not a conservative at 35 you have no brain." As wonderful as it may sound to be able to give everybody in society a free ride on the Government it is simply just not possible to do. The British Prime Minister Margaret Thatcher once stated,

> "The problem with socialism is that you eventually run out of other people's money."

History has repeated itself time and again and has proven that socialism cannot be sustained. The first socialistic failure was the Soviet Union and more recently the socialistic approach was tried by Israel, India and the United Kingdom. Socialism is based on the premise that the Government can make better decisions for the people than they can make for themselves according to Lee Edwards, Ph. D. a leading historian of American conservatism. [11]

I will end this chapter by giving you one example of liberalism that can be seen all over our country. I know a couple that are both disabled due to various ailments not brought on by them. The husband has been on disability for several years now, but since the amount that a disabled person draws is not enough to support a family the wife has continued to work. She worked herself so hard trying to help ends meet that she is now also disabled. However, since her husband was making more money when he was working than she did and he already draws disability, her disability claim was denied because they were married. After fighting this for a year or so they decided the only way they would be able to survive was for them to divorce so they could both draw the disability that they had earned. Yes I said the disability that they had earned. Disability is social security and social security is paid for by those who have worked and earned it. Social security disability is an insurance that these people paid for the whole time they were working and now that it is time collect on their investment the Government is forcing them to divorce in order to get what they paid for. What kind of Government works this way? I will tell you, it is the kind that gives away so much support to those who didn't earn it that they can't afford to give it to those who did. They are telling us now that social security is in trouble and will soon

---

[11] Three Nations That Tried Socialism and Rejected it, A commentary by Lee Edwards Oct 16, 2019

run out of funds and not be able to go on as it is. What they aren't telling you is one of the reasons that it is that condition is because the politicians have rob social security blind to pay for other things it was never intended for.

A Christian should vote for someone who supports Capitalism, and not Democratic Socialism. We all believe that people who are not able to support themselves should get help from the Government, but not those who could take care of themselves but won't do it. I believe that if a man will not work neither should he eat. I believe the economy thrives under Capitalism and grows weaker under socialistic policies. I believe that the main reason for the average person's decline financially in the last few years is inflation. The cost of living seen in every aspect of life has gone up so much in the last couple of years that the average person cannot afford to live. Yes, Covid 19 may be partially responsible, but that doesn't explain the rise in the cost of fuel, the cost of groceries, the cost of insurance and the over inflated price of housing. The average credit card interest rate is now over 21%. The interest on home loans is 8 %. The house payments that would have been $1200.00 a month a couple of years ago, are now over $2700.00 a month. Call it inflation, call it out of control spending, call it covid, or anything else you want. To the average American it is called starvation, homelessness and desperation. I will not say it is President Biden's fault, but it did happen under his watch and his economic policies have not helped the average American. We must vote for a person that will honour the promises that we have made to those who have earned their disability and social security retirement insurance and stop giving money away to those who have not done anything to earn it unless they are not able to support themselves.

CHAPTER EIGHTEEN
SUMMARY AND CONCLUSION

THE LEGISLATION OF IMMORALITY

Politicians often make the comment that you can't legislate morality. I find that remark rather interesting since the truth is almost all of our laws are based on morals straight from the Bible and therefore almost all of them could be considered the legislation of morality. Morality is simply another word for living a life that does not offend or cause harm to others. Another way of saying moral is ethical. The laws of the Bible are intended for three basic purposes. First they are for protecting a person's relationship between them and God as in the first five of the Ten Commandments. The second is to protect people from one another as in the second five of the Ten Commandments. Third, the law was intended to point out the fact the we are all guilty of breaking the laws of God at one time or another and therefore we are all in the need of a redeemer. The problem is that there is no neutrality when it comes to the law. It must take a side of right or wrong. If there is no distinction between right and wrong, then there is no need for laws at all. There are only two choices here, you either have to legislate morality or you have to legislate the opposite which is the legislation of immorality. What exactly does that look like? We are seeing this today in our society. The legislation of immorality is when Christians are being legally punished for having moral standards and refusing to participate in any activity that goes against their Christian convictions.

A GODLESS NATION

If we, as a nation, have decided to take the road away from God, then we are headed in the right direction. If this is not the case and the Christians are once again ready to take the reins, then we must put Christians in office. I find it interesting that we still have God on our money. We still swear in on the Bible in the court houses. We still see the words "In God we trust" on the back of our police cars. Our Presidents and other politicians still say God bless America, but they don't really believe what they are saying. If they did they would not be passing laws that are as anti-God as you can possibly get. We want to claim God for His blessings, but we don't want godly laws and we don't want God in our schools and we don't want God to have any influence on our politicians. God doesn't want lip service; He got plenty of that from the religious leaders in Jesus' day. These people are only calling on God and claiming to believe in God in order to look good for the Christians in our nation. In my opinion, you absolutely cannot be a Christian and take a pro-choice stand on abortion. When you remove God from the leadership of the nation, then you are left with a Godless nation. Christians should vote for Christian leadership in the White House. They should vote for Christian laws and policies. They should support Christian politicians.

CHRISTIANS HAVE RIGHTS TOO

The Constitution of the United States was based on Christian principles.

I recently read an article by the Freedom from Religion Foundation that attempted to suggest that America was not founded on Christian principles because the founding Fathers of our nation were not professing followers of Christ, even though they made numerous references to God in their declarations. This professor went on and on in his efforts to discredit Christianity by expounding on the religious backgrounds of each of these founding fathers. He argued that these men were Deist and Unitarians, but never professed to be Christians. It is, in my opinion, very easy to refute this ridiculous argument. It is obvious; both in the original documents, as well as in this professor's own words, that these men did believe in God and that many of the principles from which the nation was founded on were a product of these beliefs. Whether these men believed that their God's name was Jehovah or that He had a son named Jesus Christ at the time or not is irrelevant since the only true God is Jehovah (Jn 17:1-5), and Christ is God in the flesh (1 Tim 3:16). If that is true, then are not godly principles the same as Christian principles? It therefore is illogical to suggest that America is founded on godly principles but not Christian principles since both are based on the Bible and Jesus is God.

> These words spake Jesus, and lifted up his eyes to heaven, and said, Father, the hour

is come; glorify thy Son, that thy Son also may glorify thee: As thou hast given him power over all flesh, that he should give eternal life to as many as thou hast given him. And this is life eternal, that they might know thee the only true God, and Jesus Christ, whom thou hast sent. I have glorified thee on the earth: I have finished the work which thou gavest me to do. And now, O Father, glorify thou me with thine own self with the glory which I had with thee before the world was. (John 17:1-5)

And without controversy great is the mystery of godliness: God was manifest in the flesh, justified in the Spirit, seen of angels, preached unto the Gentiles, believed on in the world, received up into glory. (1Tim 3:16)

One of those principles is the right to practice our Christianity without fear or restrictions from the Government. Today, everyone in America seems to be granted this right of religious freedom except the Christians whom are the ones that guaranteed this right to begin with. We as Christians do not wish to prevent anyone else from practicing their religion in any way that they want provided that it doesn't prevent us from following our own convictions. This is what laws are for. Today Christians are being singled out for having convictions against certain human rights. We believe that other people's human rights are just fine with us provided that it doesn't keep us from practicing our rights. The laws are becoming more and more in favor of human rights rather than religious freedoms. We don't believe we should be forced to participate in other peoples unrighteous activities at the expense of our own convictions and religious freedoms. We must follow the laws based on Romans chapter thirteen, but that doesn't mean we should just lay down and take it without any verbal and political opposition. The only way to ensure that Christians will be allowed to keep their religious freedoms is to keep Christians, or at least those with Christian morals in office. When I told people I was going to write a book on religion and politics they all looked at me and said something like, "you're really looking for trouble aren't you". No, I'm really not, but I think it is time for Christians to take a stand and get our nation headed back in the right direction. A quote that is generally attributed to Edmund Burke is:

> "The only thing necessary for the triumph of evil is for good men to do nothing"

CHRISTIAN PRINCIPLES

I want to address some of those Christian principles that I believe are being attacked.

INCOME EQUALITY

One of our largest political parties pushes the agenda of income equality. Just from the introduction and the title one should be able to tell that this is not talking about all people having the same opportunity to succeed. We all believe this is true. Everyone in America has the same opportunity to do all that they can with the abilities that they were born with. Not every person ever born is born with the same abilities or the same potential for success, but they all have what God planned for them to have. Christians have made it clear that we believe that all people are created equal in the eyes of God and we believe that they should all have rights in the sight of the Government. Just because people have equal rights doesn't mean they are automatically entitled to equal income. In a Capitalistic society such as the United States, all people have equal rights and all people have equal opportunity, but they never will have equal abilities or attributes that lead to financial success. Financial success is not and should not be determined by the Government. Our unique abilities and personalities and talents are given to us by God. I believe almost everyone has a potential to be successful in one thing or another. We were not all created to perform the same functions in life or to have the same abilities and successes. Just like a man and a woman; though they are equally significant in God's plan and in our society, they are not the same. While men have more talent in some areas, women have more talent in others. All people should have the same access to opportunity, but only God can determine who will be able to take advantage of those opportunities. In political circles income equality is the policy of taking from the successful to give to the unsuccessful. Personally I would not consider a free handout the same as income that I worked for and earned, but these people do. Many of the proposed policies from all political parties are just intended to offer incentives

BUYING VOTES

Many of the proposed policies from all political parties are just intended to be incentives to buy votes. The way our Government works is any political party that expects to make any significant changes in the way things are run must spend an enormous amount of money and time to gain votes. This is because the only way to maintain power, which means the ability to change laws, is to remain in power. Because of this, many laws are passed that are bad for America, but they are considered to be popular to win certain votes from certain groups. Some politicians vote for leaner laws on drugs because it is popular with the younger electorate. Some vote for laws that favor special treatment to certain religious or racial groups in order to gain their votes. Because of this practice there are many laws active today that make no sense unless you consider who they benefit. This is simply buying votes and a Christian should be very careful when casting their ballots and not vote for anyone who has shown a tendency to be persuaded to vote in favor of a particular group and going against God's laws in the process. Most politicians do not care about what God says only what the voters say. One of the reasons we are in this predicament is because the majority of Christians do not bother to vote anymore. In order to change this trend we must get out and vote and make our voices heard. This is the only thing that will change the ungodly trend we are caught in.

ELECTABILITY

Another thing to keep in mind when casting your vote is electability. This has never been so prevalent as it is today. There are a lot of things that I liked about President Trumps policies. I believe for the most part, he had good intentions and was headed in the right direction to get our country back on track with God. On the other hand, the liberals have been fairly successful in ruining his reputation for everyone except those on the far right. I'm not going to say that anyone should or should not vote a certain way, but I will say that President Trump has caused a lot of damage to his own reputation with all liberals and many moderate conservatives with his lack of presidential representation. I cannot think of any President that we have had in my lifetime that has acted less presidential. Personally I like his stand on many political issues, but I'm not certain that he is capable of winning another election at this point. Of course things can change between now and Election Day so we will have to see how he comes out with his legal difficulties. Personally I think the majority of his legal difficulties are just drummed up charges by political opposition that would rather destroy him legally than face him politically. If the Party could nominate in the primaries, someone who had Trump's policies but not his temperament this person might be more electable in a general election.

WHAT SHOULD OUR VOTES BE BASED ON?

As a Christian our votes should be based on the Biblical answers to political policies, laws, positions and issues. Following I will touch on just a few of these:

1. Pro-life (abortion)- According to the Bible life begins at conception and according to our Constitution all people are created equal and have the same right to life. Anyone who does not believe this is not worthy of the Christian vote.

2. What is Democratic Socialism- Democratic socialism is still socialism with some democratic principles applied. In any case it is still socialism and we have already seen that socialism is not sustainable. Capitalism is what made our country great and it is what best affords each person the equal opportunity to succeed.

3. Gay Rights (Same Sex Marriage) - I am not opposed to people expressing themselves personally. I tell people that the LBGTQ lifestyle is a sin. I do not hate the sinner I hate the sin because it destroys people. The problem with same sex marriage is it has resulted in the criminalization of Christianity as Christians only want the right to refuse to participate in actives that are abhorrent to God.

4. The Fight against Terrorism- The fight against terrorism is difficult because when it is pointed out that certain groups of people have terroristic intentions and

should be watched and treated differently than other groups it is suggested that they are being discriminated against. These predictions are not based on prejudice, but rather statistical fact. I'm not suggesting that all Muslims should be considered terrorist. I am saying that when a certain group has been identified as producing terroristic cells that they should be subject to certain restrictions in order to protect the general public. This is not prejudice, this is common sense. I believe our most prominent threat pertaining to terrorism right now is President Biden's open border policies. In order to protect America from this thereat the borders must be secured if it isn't already too late.

5. Number One Crisis Today- I believe our number one crisis today is the unprovoked attack on Israel by the Hamas on October 7th, 2023 killing over 1400 people and taking hundreds of hostages. The struggles between Israel and the Hamas have been going on for years. This time Israel insists they will not stop until the Hamas no longer exist. Since the beginning of the war Israel has been retaliating relentlessly and it is causing outrage in the rest of the world because of the civilian casualties in Gaza. The Hamas continually points to Israel insisting that these casualties are due to the brutality of the Israelis, but it was the Hamas that started the conflict and it is Hamas that is causing the civilian casualties by hiding their forces among the Palestinian people, even in civilian hospitals. It is only a matter of time until President Biden will stop defending the actions of the Israelites and join the rest of the world in their condemnation of Israel. The president

has already joined with other nations in calling for a cease fire. Israel says this is enough; there will be no ceasefire this time until the Hamas is soundly defeated. The Bible tells us that God will stand by Israel until the end and He has done it before repeatedly. America must stand by Israel.

6. The national debt- The National Debt must be repaid. With all of the other issues facing our nation today the national debt continues to be ignored and the debt goes up and up. I'm not blaming this debt on any particular political party since it has been constantly on the rise since President Bush and has been totally ignored by presidents from both parties since then. The thing is, we as Christians should know that the borrower is slave to the lender and we should owe no man anything. The only way this will ever be addressed is by electing someone who actually cares about the burden that we are placing on our children. We should be leaving investments for our children not more debt. We are now at 33 trillion dollars in debt. This is a number that is unimaginable to the average citizen. Most believe it is irrelevant because it will never be paid. At this rate America will be owned by its lenders and our society as we know it will cease to exist. We must vote for a candidate that will at least display a concern about this debt and have a plan to address it.

7. Gun violence- This is probably one of the most controversial issues in politics. The fact is that gun violence is a major problem in America and everybody

knows it. The question is what the proper way to resolve it is. The far right is against any firearm restrictions due to the fear that once that door is opened the left will impose laws that will take guns away from everyone. I showed you earlier that the Bible supports the right and even encourages the right for citizens to own weapons intended to defend their families. It is a man's responsibility to protect his family and in our society today that would be hard to do without a gun since everybody has one. I believe if you outlaw guns only outlaws will have guns. Besides all of that the second amendment to the Constitution guarantees the citizens of America the right to keep and bear arms. I think the problem needs to be addressed by finding ways to keep guns away from criminals and the mentally ill without disarming law abiding citizens.

8. The Drug Problem- I have already revealed the seriousness of drug and alcohol abuse in American cities. Who is to blame? The open borders, the rise in crime, the decriminalization of drugs, the prosecution of the police officers, the overcrowding of the prisons resulting in allowing criminals to avoid prosecution and go free, the so-called sanctuary cities that sacrifice the safety of their law abiding citizens to protect the human rights of illegal aliens. Illegal aliens are criminals by definition. I don't care if this is politically correct or not. They are not just immigrants if they come here illegally. All of these things are contributors to the overall drug abuse problem, but what does it come down to? Lawlessness expressed in many different forms is the reason that drugs are such a large

problem in our country today. We don't even need to pass new laws. We only need to enforce the ones that we already have and back the police instead of prosecuting them for doing their job. I'm not saying there aren't any bad law enforcement officers, I'm certain there are; however, the overwhelming majority of the time these people would not be in the positions they are in with the law if they weren't breaking the law to begin with. The Bible requires Christians to be on the side of the law since God is the one that allows them to be in power and therefore we must support the police as well. In my opinion the enforcement of the law is the solution to lawlessness in many forms including the abuse of drugs and alcohol.

9. Climate Change- This used to be called global warming but the extreme cold weather patterns in the recent past forced them to change it to climate change. The far right will tell you this is all a hoax, but even those without another agenda will have enough common sense to know that something is wrong with this theory. I will not go into all the reasons for that statement here since we have already talked about it in detail. The basic argument for Christians is the fact that the earth was created for man not man for the earth. In fact so were the vegetation and the wildlife. They were all created to support mankind and are here for that purpose. It is not that the Christian doesn't care about the environment, which is a false statement. The issue is when laws are passed that cause people to suffer in order to preserve the things that were created for people to begin with. We need to vote for someone

who will be concerned about the environment, but will not pass laws that will harm people to protect the environment. We need to find ways to protect the environment while helping people instead of hurting them.

10. The economy and inflation- Tell the truth, do you feel better off economically today than you did under the Trump Presidency? There are numerous reasons why our economy, in the eyes of the average American, is worse off now than then. In the mean time President Biden consistently touts about his economic achievements while the average American is not convinced. I believe the main reason for this is the unbelievable inflation resulting in a cost of living that most Americans can't afford. Everything has gone up except the pay. I know I don't know a lot about the control of the economy, but to me raising interest rates on everything at the same time that everything else has skyrocketed has only compounded the problem. Americans are further and further in debt because the only way they can survive is to live on credit with the hope that it will get better soon.

THE LIBERAL PHILOSOPHY VERSES THE CONSERVATIVE PHILOSOPHY

I'm not going to tell you which political party you should affiliate yourself with, but I think it should be the one that best promotes the Christian principles, morals and values that we have been talking about. Personally I wish there were no political party's only individuals that were free to express themselves based on their personal beliefs and convictions. Today the Democratic Party is something totally different than it was 20 years ago. Some may like the way it has gone and some will not. The Republican Party has also become so fractured that it is difficult to determine where it stands on many issues. In either case, the only way it is going to get better for the Christian and for the nation is for Christians to stand up and make their voices heard. Choose a candidate that best represents these issues on the side of godliness and righteousness and commit. The liberal philosophy is the Robin Hood approach; that is to steal from the rich and give to the poor. Even though it may sound reasonable on the surface it results in the implementation of Democratic socialism and the destruction of Capitalism. If this is the direction you want our country to head in then by all means let it reflect in your ballot. If however, you believe in free enterprise and a Capitalistic society, which is the view of the conservative Christian, then, cast your vote with that in mind. Regardless of your choice this book is intended to point out the views of the conservative Christian and lay out the reasons for these convictions. It is also designed to encourage everyone to get out and vote regardless of what your political views are. I believe we are still a Christian nation and I believe we will prove it in the near future.

The only danger with voting policy instead of party is the influence the party may have on that person once they have been elected. It is difficult for an elected official to go against the wishes of the party that they represent and stay in office.

Regardless of your political affiliation I pray that God will bless you and your family and will give you the guidance of the Holy Spirit in the coming elections. As Christians we must follow the law and pray for our appointed officials.

Sincerely your humble servant
David Boudreaux

www.ingramcontent.com/pod-product-compliance
Lightning Source LLC
LaVergne TN
LVHW050024080526
838202LV00069B/6902